The Insanely Practical Guide
to
Reloading Ammunition

The Insanely Practical Guide to Reloading Ammunition

Learn the easy way
to reload your own
rifle and pistol cartridges

Tom McHale

Insanely Practical Guides

Also by Tom McHale

The Rookie's Guide to Guns and Shooting, Handgun Edition
The Rookie's Guide to the Springfield Armory XD-S
The Insanely Practical Guide to Gun Holsters, 2nd Edition

Published by Insanely Practical Guides, Charleston, SC
Printed in the United States of America.

ISBN 978-0-9890652-8-3
Digital Edition ISBN 978-0-9890652-9-0

CONTENTS

But First, A Serious Note!

Reloading your own ammunition is fun, rewarding and potentially addictive!

But, like anything related to shooting, it's serious business.

I don't have a lawyer, but if I did, I am sure he would tell me to tell you to exercise extreme caution when it comes to reloading.

Always, always, always stick to published load data guidelines. Don't guess, estimate, or create your own loads outside of published limits. Brass centerfire ammunition for rifles and handguns generates pressures in the tens of thousands of pounds per square inch, and you definitely don't want to exceed safe pressure limits while shooting.

This book does not include load recipes by design. Powder, projectile and reloading equipment companies produce excellent publications with proven and tested safe load data, so we won't try to replicate that here.

We try to make the shooting world more accessible and understandable with a little humor now and then, and we work hard to make complex topics like ammunition reloading simple to understand. Use this guide as an educational tool to help you understand some of the basics and the reloading steps, but always rely on published reloading data as the final authority when it comes to specifics.

This book is written in literary assault format for your enjoyment— half-cocked, but right on target. I hope that doesn't offend your sense of decency and decorum — too much.

Chapter One

INTRODUCTION

I picked up the ammunition reloading bug about fifteen years ago — most likely by contact from a copy of the *Lyman Reloading Handbook* at a local gun show. Who knows where that book was before I touched it?

Since that day, I've reloaded billions and billions of rounds of rifle and pistol ammunition. Well, maybe not billions, but certainly enough to cause two-thirds of the members of Congress to scamper off to their therapist's office or the nearest pub.

What do I have to show for it?

> ▷ Two children who have become expert shooters. I believe this is partly a result of consuming the ammunition I painstakingly reload at a rate comparable to that which the space shuttle's main engine consumes liquid hydrogen.

▷ 32 metric tons of projectiles in 25 different calibers — all ready to reload. These are stored in the workroom in my garage. While this is my "happy place" it's not popular with other family members who would also like to store things in the climate-controlled garage space. As these projectiles are made mostly of lead, the earth in this part of the country has been compacted to 17 feet below sea level.

▷ 93,452 spent brass cartridge cases picked up in the aftermath of my kids' shooting and that of others too lazy to pick up their own brass.

▷ Lots of reloading toys!

▷ Critically important knowledge that will come in handy when the Zombie Apocalypse happens and ammunition reloaders are treated like 13th century sorcerers. You can call us Merlin.

▷ Thousands of hours of productive relaxation. Productive relaxation you say? What on earth is that? It's when you do something for the joy of it, and end up with a happy ending — in this case lots of ammunition.

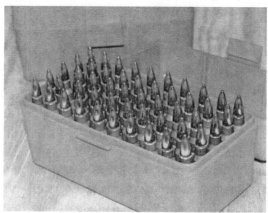

Making this is fun, satisfying, and for me, relaxing.

Reloading is a great hobby if you're cut out to enjoy that sort of thing. Yes, you can save money, but the real fun is the process, and the satisfaction of being able to create the perfect ammunition for any of your firearms. Want less recoil in your competition pistol? No problem! Want to get your bolt-action rifle to shoot one half inch groups at 100 yards? No problem, assuming your rifle is up to the task. Want to hunt with ammunition you made yourself? Got that covered!

There are plenty of reasons to reload your own ammunition. Hopefully this book will help you uncover which ones are important to you.

WHY YOU NEED THIS BOOK - AND A COUPLE OF OTHERS

This book has a simple mission: to help you learn how to reload your own centerfire ammunition and avoid some of the pitfalls that plague every new ammunition reloader.

Notice I specified centerfire ammunition. That's standard rifle and pistol ammo with brass cartridge cases. Rimfire ammunition, like .22 Long Rifle, .22 Magnum and .17 HMR is not reloadable as it does not use a removable primer. Shotgun ammunition is reloadable too, but the process is significantly different, so this book won't address it. Count on us writing The Insanely Practical Guide to Reloading Shotgun Ammunition in the future.

Left to right: .22 long rifle rimfire, .22 Magnum rimfire, 9mm centerfire (notice the primer in the base) and 12 gauge shotgun, also centerfire.

When I started reloading, I made lots of mistakes. I learned the hard way by screwing things up on occasion. Yes, I had fun, but my learning process might have been more fun if someone had taken the time to explain the procedures and equipment to me. In plain non-engineering oriented English.

Fortunately, that's what we do here at Insanely Practical Guides. Nothing would make us happier than to have a million or so folks start reloading their own ammunition.

This book is not a reloading manual. Great companies like Hornady, Sierra, Lyman and others publish those. They invest millions of dollars in fancy equipment like ballistic test barrels, strain gauges, piezo transducers and plenty of Cheezy Poofs and Red Bull for the lab staff — all to develop safe and tested load recipes.

This book is an instructional guide that will walk you through the steps of reloading your own ammunition in a fun, and more importantly, easy to understand way. Reloading manuals are great resources for understanding safe and tested load recipes. While most include an introductory section that talks about the reloading process and equipment, none that I've found show you, step by step, exactly how to do it in an easy to understand way.

When you start reloading more calibers, you'll want multiple manuals in your collection.

Make no mistake, you need a reloading manual — preferably several.

Think of reloading manuals as sheet music. And this book as Mrs. Clutterbuck's piano lessons you took in third grade. If you develop a sudden urge to play Carnegie Hall, or even Bodean's Wet Whistle Bar and Bait Shop, you could just order sheet music from the internet. But it probably wouldn't be the most direct path to ivory key success. Take some lessons first, then order the sheet music. We'll all thank you!

Although we think reading this book will be a far more pleasant experience than weekly lessons in Mrs. Clutterbuck's den, the idea is the same. We'll teach you how to do the steps. Then you're off to fame, fortune and custom ammunition.

Chapter Two

SHOULD YOU RELOAD YOUR OWN AMMUNITION?

While I can spend hours fantasizing about all the cool gadgets like case concentricity gauges in the Sinclair Reloading catalog, others may have more traditional interests, like gardening, golfing or scrapbooking.

To decide whether reloading ammunition is something you should do, consider the following:

YOU'LL SAVE MONEY.

If you reload for fun and don't place a dollar value on your reloading time, your cost per cartridge will almost certainly be lower than the price of factory ammunition. That's because you are only paying for the parts and not the labor. And the most expensive part, the cartridge case, is reusable. Of course, you have to reload often enough to cover the start-up equipment costs.

Let's look at a simple example. Right now, .223 practice ammo costs somewhere around $0.45 to $0.50 per round. If you reload it yourself, plan on spending about $0.09 per bullet, $0.03 per primer and $0.08 for each powder charge. If you have to buy brass, you can use each casing about 10 times, so your per use cost is about $0.04. That brings us to about $0.24 per round, not counting your time. Yeah, I know. You know a guy who can get all this stuff cheaper. Keep in mind, this is just a rough estimate

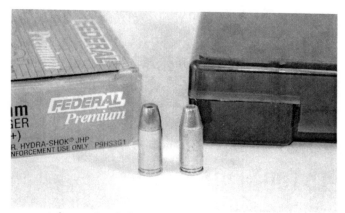

A factory loaded 9mm and a hand reloaded 9mm.

example for those who are uninitiated.

So, not counting labor and the initial equipment investment, you might plan on producing your own ammunition at about half the cost of factory ammunition. Of course, the cost varies depending on caliber and which components you use. When you get really hooked, you can buy components by the truckload and reduce your costs dramatically. Of course, you'll be storing mountains of primers, powder and projectiles.

YOU WON'T SAVE MONEY, YOU'LL SPEND MORE MONEY.

Once you start reloading, you'll want to get all the gear. Like digital scales, electronic powder dispensers, power case trimmers, progressive reloading presses, and custom reloading benches. You'll also shoot a lot

Save money? Well, sort of. If you don't count all the accessories you'll want to buy!

more, so even though your cost per round might be lower, you can easily end up spending more money overall.

Many reloaders like to say that they don't save any money, per se, but they get to shoot more for the same amount of money. Make sense?

ARE YOU, OR CAN YOU BE, DETAIL-ORIENTED?

As with any shooting related activity, safety comes first. Like shooting, reloading is perfectly safe, as long as you pay attention and follow the rules—every time, without fail. With reloading, you have to pay close attention to all aspects of the task — very, very carefully.

You'll need to be cognizant of the exact type and amount of powder placed in each cartridge. Undercharging (not using enough powder) and overcharging (using too much powder) are equally dangerous. Both can result in a damaged gun and physical injury.

Attention to detail is really, really important. Once out the box, these primers may look identical, but they're not — and bad things can happen if you don't keep them straight.

You'll need to pay close attention to be sure that each projectile is seated exactly the same way, and at the exact right depth. Pushing projectiles too far into the cartridge case can increase pressure to dangerous levels. A little error can mean a lot of trouble!

Using the right components from professionally published recipes is mandatory. There's no room for distractions that might cause you to load the wrong primer, powder or projectile.

While reloading may sound scary, as long as you are careful and attentive, you can manufacture safe and reliable ammunition.

IT'S A GATEWAY DRUG.

You know, like crystal meth. Once you start on that stuff, you'll quickly move to something really serious! Likewise, if you start reloading something simple, like pistol cartridges, you'll soon move to rifle cartridges. Before you know it, you'll be melting lead in your kitchen and casting your own bullets. And we all know how much other family members enjoy lead fumes in the kitchen.

If you start to reload, be prepared to go deep. You just might become an addict too. Fortunately, reloading addictions rarely lead to family troubles or job loss.

WHAT'S YOUR TIME WORTH?

In our .223 Remington example, we figured we might save about $0.25 per round, not counting the value of your time. So on a per-round basis, your time needs to be worth less than $0.25 for the amount of time it takes to assemble one round, or else you're unprofitable — like the Federal Government.

As you develop basic reloading skills, you can figure out how long it takes you to assemble one round of ammo. But, time value calculations are tricky because they depend on the equipment you have and the pace at which you work safely. Progressive reloading press manufacturers claim ammunition output numbers in the neighborhood of 500 rounds per hour, but that doesn't count other chores like case preparation.

So, applying some hard core financial analysis to the value of your time, if you spend most of your waking hours hanging out at Occupy Something Evil Protests, you're probably in good shape. If you have a paying job, chances are you're not beating the ammunition manufacturers in the hourly wage efficiency game. You might be better off working more to cover your ammo bills. But then you would miss out on the joy and relaxation of ammunition reloading, wouldn't you?

DO YOU SHOOT OFTEN, OR DO YOU WANT TO SHOOT MORE OFTEN?

Reloading only makes sense economically if you'll do it frequently and with enough volume to recover your investment in reloading equipment. Like most other new endeavors, there's also a learning curve that will cost you some time.

If you shoot a lot, or want to shoot a lot more, then these investments in time and equipment won't be such a big deal.

DO YOU LIKE TO TINKER?

As you're probably starting to see, it doesn't make a whole lot of sense to take up reloading if you absolutely hate the activity. If you value your time accurately, you're not really saving money, so you better enjoy doing it. Those big expensive ammunition manufacturing plants do a pretty good job of producing quality ammunition at the lowest possible price. But if you consider time spent as an enjoyable hobby, you can have fun, and shoot more frequently, at the lowest-possible component cost.

If you really enjoy the tinkering process, learning to reload will allow you to do things like make 37 different varieties of ammunition for your .30-06 rifle. Or pistol rounds for your Glock 17 that meet 5 different power factors. Or perhaps you'd like to create "no recoil loads" for that old military rifle that's been passed down. If you're a born tinkerer, all these things, and more, are possible.

DO YOU COMPETE?

Making your own cartridges can help you keep up with the volume of ammo required for shooting competitions without breaking the bank. Better yet, you can create a custom load that works in your specific gun, meets the required power factor, yet minimizes recoil for fast follow-up shots. My young nephews love shooting my full-size Springfield Armory 1911 with wimpy plinking loads—it gives them great bragging rights with their friends.

If you want to get into rifle competitions, reloading your own ammo, customized to your rifle, is almost a must. Half the fun is trying to one-up the other competitors with better ammunition right?

DO YOU SHOOT RIFLES? DO YOU HAVE ONE OR MORE UNUSUAL GUNS?

Pistol rounds have a small per-cartridge component cost benefit, but rifle reloading can have a huge cost per round benefit. My eye-opening experience came when my son bought a 1938 Arisaka. At the time, factory loads were over $2.00 each. By reloading my own, I was able to bring the cost per round down to about $0.35.

There are plenty of rifles and pistols like the Arisaka that use rare and expensive ammunition. Assuming your guns are modern and built for standard smokeless ammunition, they might be great candidates for reloading.

DO YOU LIVE FOR ACCURACY BRAGGING RIGHTS?

Factory produced ammunition is excellent, and we have no intention of portraying it as anything less. But, by necessity, factory ammunition must be made within acceptable ranges of dimension specifications so it will function in a broad array of rifles or pistols made by many different manufacturers. As a result, there's a limit to the accuracy performance you can achieve with your specific rifle. If you're loading for one specific rifle, you can push the dimension envelope a bit and find the best possible performance for your gun.

Details matter when it comes to repeatable accuracy. You can tune a specific projectile, case, powder, primer, and seating depth combination that wrings every bit of potential accuracy from your rifle.

DO YOU HUNT?

It's satisfying to make your own custom crafted ammunition and use it in the field. With hundreds of projectile designs on the market, you can create a load with the exact performance you want for your intended game.

DO YOU HAVE KIDS?

As I have found out, my kids are capable of maintaining a constant cyclic rate of fire of just over 42,358 rounds per minute with my sons DPMS A3 Lite AR-15 rifle. Doing some quick math, I might spend three times the national debt to buy their ammo.

DOES YOUR FAMILY LIKE YOU?

Or would they prefer that you hibernate more often? When you get the reloading bug, you'll find all sorts of excuses to hide away in your reloading space for hours on end. As you can tell, I'm a reloading fanatic, so I've already made a decision in favor of reloading. Why? Because time won't waste itself.

What do you think? Is reloading for you? If you think so, read on. We'll get you started in no time!

Chapter Three

THE PROCESS OF RELOADING

We're dedicating a chapter to each step in the reloading process. But first, it's important to have an idea of the overall flow, so a conversation about each step will make more sense.

But first, just to clear up some of the key parts and terms, we'll take a brief look at the anatomy of a cartridge.

Then we'll take a walk through the process of reloading basic pistol cartridges. After that, I'll point out a couple of differences in the process of reloading rifle cartridges.

ANATOMY OF A CARTRIDGE

Think of a cartridge as a completed assembly. People might call them bullets, but that technically only refers to the projectile that leaves the gun.

A centerfire cartridge is made of four components: primer, cartridge case, powder (or propellant) and the projectile itself. For reloading purposes, the only part of a cartridge that is reusable is the brass cartridge case.

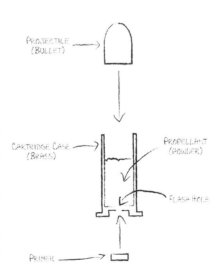

PROJECTILE
(BULLET)

CARTRIDGE CASE
(BRASS)

PROPELLANT
(POWDER)

FLASH HOLE

PRIMER

Primer

The primer is a small metal "cap" coated on the interior side with explosive. The primer itself is constructed with an internal "anvil" that helps crush the priming compound to cause chemical ignition. This shower of burning material is what passes through the primer flash hole in the bottom of a cartridge case to ignite the propellant. Many primers are made from lead styphnate although lead-free primers are used in some cases.

SAFETY FIRST!

Exercise extreme caution when handling primers! They are designed to explode when struck by a firing pin. As such, they can explode from other forms of contact. Always wear safety glasses when reloading or working with primers!

Also, many primers use lead styphnate, which can result in airborne lead — especially at indoor shooting ranges. Always wash your hands after shooting or working with primers.

There are different types and sizes of primers. The purposes of this book, just know that there are large and small pistol primers and large and small rifle primers. Within these four types are additional varieties like magnum, bench rest, military and more. Your reloading manual will tell you exactly which type of primer to use for a given cartridge.

Cartridge Case

The cartridge case, or, as reloaders call it, the brass, is the casing that holds the primer, propellant and projectile. For centerfire cartridges, the case will have a primer pocket in the base with a small "flash hole" connecting that to the interior body of the cartridge case. Bullets are seated in the mouth of the case.

The case is the only reusable part of a cartridge, assuming you're not digging up fired bullets, remelting and molding them.

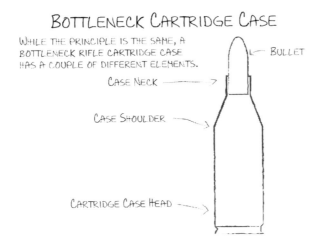

BOTTLENECK CARTRIDGE CASE

WHILE THE PRINCIPLE IS THE SAME, A
BOTTLENECK RIFLE CARTRIDGE CASE
HAS A COUPLE OF DIFFERENT ELEMENTS.

BULLET

CASE NECK

CASE SHOULDER

CARTRIDGE CASE HEAD

Actually, that's a reloading option too! Of course, the propellant (powder) is consumed and the primer is a one-time bang affair.

Propellant / Powder

There are a hundred or so types and brands of propellant powders available to reloaders. For simplicity, we'll just refer to them as powders in the remainder of this book, as propellant sounds very NASA-like. And this is a practical guide, not an engineering epistle.

Anyway, the reason for so many different powder options is to provide different rates of burn. From chemical composition and/or shape of the powder flakes, sticks or little balls, powders can be made that burn faster or slower. The speed at which powder burns does not equate to bullet velocity. Rather, it optimizes the gas pressure and time curve to most efficiently launch a bullet of a given weight downrange. A small pistol cartridge like the .32

ACP may use a fast burning powder, yet launch a bullet at only 800 feet per second. A big .30-06 rifle cartridge may use a slower burning powder, yet launch its projectile at over 2,700 feet per second. There's a lot of science that we'll get into more in the *Powder Charging* chapter.

Projectile

The projectile, or the bullet, is the only part that exits the muzzle of your gun. The powder is consumed, the primer smashed up somewhat and the (now empty) brass case is ejected either manually or automatically.

RELOADING STEPS: STRAIGHT WALL PISTOL CALIBERS

Components of a rifle cartridge, right to left: Primer, cartridge case, powder and projectile. Handgun cartridges have the same components.

When you boil all the complexity down, reloading is simply recycling fired cartridges. Just like plastic milk containers, but a lot less smelly. For most modern ammunition types, a cartridge is composed of several components — some of which are expendable and others reusable.

Let's take an insanely practical look at the steps involved in reloading straight wall handgun ammunition, like 9mm, .40 Smith & Wesson, .38 Special or .45 ACP. Later on we'll talk more about the basic equipment you need to do this.

But first…

If there is the slightest chance you might take up reloading in the future, there is a pre-step. Hoard brass! Yes, like that show on A&E. Hoard brass until you're living room is knee deep and the dog can't makes its way to the kitchen. Why? You'll need it. And it's expensive. Every time you bend over to pick up a casing, think $0.10 to $0.75! You'd pick up a quarter or two every time you saw one on the ground right?

1. Inspect and clean the brass

The circle of life: Loaded cartridge, spent brass, primer has been removed, new primer installed, ready for powder, seating a new bullet, and completed cartridge.

Technically, you don't have to clean brass cartridge casings to reload them, but I always do. Cleaning the brass helps you make nice, pretty ammunition that is sure to impress your friends. More importantly, it reduces the risk of your reloading dies getting all gunked up. Clean ammunition also feeds into your gun more reliably.

2. Remove the spent primers

The primer is one of the expendable items. Once it's blown up, it's no good anymore. Either a dedicated decapping die is used to punch the old primer out of the bottom of the casing, or more commonly, the die that resizes your brass will also knock the old primer out.

3. Resize the cartridge case

When you fire a rifle or handgun cartridge, the whole brass casing actually expands in the chamber of the gun. As the pressure goes down when the bullet leaves the barrel, the brass shrinks back a bit, thereby allowing extraction from the chamber and ejection right at the person standing to your immediate right. While it shrinks, it doesn't shrink all the way back to original size. A resizing die is used to "encourage by brute force" the brass back into the correct exterior dimensions. This step ensures that your reloaded ammunition will fit back into the chamber of your gun and fire properly.

4. Belling the case mouth

While this sounds like a boxing move, it simply means opening up the opening of the cartridge case mouth so you can fit a new bullet in there. In the previous step, you squished the dickens out of the brass from the outside in. In this step, you "re-open" the case mouth just a little.

5. Priming the cartridge

Remember that spent primer we knocked out earlier? It's time to shove a new one in the primer pocket. The primer is what starts the whole "go bang" process, so this step is important!

6. Charging the cartridge (Adding powder)

At this point, we have clean and properly sized brass. And since we just put a new primer in, there's no longer a hole in the bottom, so we can add a new measure of powder, or as the reloading geeks call it, powder. Propellant charge is measured by weight, in grains, but the right equipment allows you to dispense the correct amount by volume.

> *Grain: While we're here, people often wonder what a grain is. While intuitively it sounds like one little speck of powder, it's actually 1/7000th of a pound. As a handgun cartridge might use four grains of powder, think of that as 0.00057142857143 pounds. It only takes a little.*

7. Seating the bullet

Seating refers to pushing the bullet into the (now slightly opened) case mouth to the proper depth. For safety reasons that we'll talk about later, and to make sure your newly manufactured cartridge will fit in your gun, the overall length of the cartridge needs to be within standard dimensions for that caliber.

8. Crimping the cartridge case

In this step, you press the brass around the case mouth back into proper shape once the bullet is seated. Remember earlier when we opened the case mouth a bit to allow for bullet insertion? This step puts things back to normal. We'll get into more detail later, but for now, just know that crimping is not what holds the bullet in place. The tension of the bullet and cartridge case interior walls does that. Crimping just evens things out and removes the belling we created.

9. Packaging and inspection!

I like to list this as the last step as it's important to check your work. For me, doing this as I put completed cartridges into containers makes sense. I look to make sure that primers are seated correctly and that bullets are seated to the right depth. The inspection steps is important for safety and reliability. You don't want to be blazing through the Smoke and Hope stage of your local Steel Challenge match when you encounter a cartridge where you forgot to insert a primer, right? That empty-sounding "click" would be embarrassing.

This sounds like a lot of steps doesn't it? It can be, but fortunately you can pay for automation. Depending on your equipment choices, many of these steps can be consolidated into a single action. We'll teach you all about that soon.

RELOADING STEPS: BOTTLENECK RIFLE CALIBERS

GUN WORDS
Explained!

Bottleneck Rifle Cartridges: Most rifle calibers use a cartridge case shaped like, wait for it, an old-fashioned Coke bottle. The bottom is larger and the case bends in as you get closer to the actual bullet. This shape allows for a lot more powder for any given bullet diameter without having to have a cartridge that's four feet long.

If you want to reload bottleneck rifle cartridges, like most rifle calibers, there are just a couple of extra steps from those we just covered for simple pistol calibers.

To keep things as simple and insanely practical as possible, we'll just cover the differences in the rifle cartridge reloading process here. The basic steps of pistol cartridge reloading still apply.

Lubricating Cases Before Resizing

For reasons we will discuss in more detail in the *Resizing Brass* chapter, you need to lubricate the outside of bottleneck rifle cases before you resize them. If you don't, they will get stuck in the resizing die, and it's kind of a pain to get them out.

Case Trimming

Due to differences in the shape of bottleneck rifle cartridges, and as a result of the resizing process, your rifle cartridges will "stretch" in length just a bit each time you fire and resize them. For ammunition that chambers and works consistently, the brass cartridge cases all need to be the same length, and within caliber specifications, before you start seating bullets. For these reasons, you will need to trim a bit off the ends of your rifle cartridges as part of the reloading process.

Chamfering and Deburring

Chamfering is a fancy word that basically means "beveling" and deburring simply means smoothing rough edges. When you cut some brass from the mouth of cartridge cases, it leaves rough edges. The chamfering step bevels and smooths the inside of the case mouth, making bullet seating easier and more consistent. The deburring step smooths the outside edges.

Lube Cleaning

When you lubricate the cases before resizing, you also need to remove the lubrication residue when you're done. Guns don't operate well when the cartridges are all oily as that interferes with the normal process of cartridge expansion and contraction in the chamber when a gun is fired. This step can be as simple as wiping the cases with a clean rag. Or you can clean them again with a tumbler.

That's about it. Reloading rifle cartridges is almost the same as straight wall pistol calibers. Don't worry, we'll get into more detail on these steps when we cover each reloading operation in detail.

Chapter Four

Basic Equipment Requirements

When you get serious enough to break out the checkbook and buy some equipment, we can help you know what you absolutely need first — and what optional gear will make your life easier. Like any activity that requires an investment in gear, there are a million and seven ways to accomplish the task with varying types of equipment. Here, we're going to focus on what I think is a reasonable tradeoff between cost and effectiveness. You can do with less, and I'll point out those areas where you can skimp. You can also make your life a lot easier by spending a few extra dollars and I'll point out those opportunities too.

For simplicity, we'll focus on reloading traditional straight-walled pistol ammunition first. Later in this chapter, I've included a section that lists the extra things you'll need to reload bottleneck rifle cartridges.

With that said, let's look at the basic equipment you need to get started.

Case Cleaner

When you pick up brass cartridge cases that have been fired, they'll be dirty. Depending on whether you shoot at an indoor or outdoor range, the relative level of "dirt" will vary. At minimum, you'll want to remove any loose powder residue and whatever dirt your brass acquired when it hit the floor. While your brass does not have to be shiny like new, it does need to have the loose dirt removed.

Yuck!

If you want to go super cheap, you can clean your brass with stuff you already have. Hot water, a plastic container and some Tide (or a mixture of dish detergent, vinegar and salt) will get the job done. Your brass won't be all pretty and shiny, but it will be clean enough to reload. To me, this is a hassle that's not worth saving sixty to eighty dollars on a...

Brass tumbler

A tumbler is simply a plastic bowl with a motor underneath that vibrates the contents. Add "tumbling media," which is a fancy term for ground up corn cobs or walnut shells, and the vibration of the brass mixed with tumbling media will get your cases clean inside and out. After it runs for a while, you simply sift the media from the brass and your cases are ready to go. Some tumblers have a sifting feature built in.

Here's something to take into consideration. I've learned the hard way that if you're going to use a dry tumbler, you really

An RCBS case tumbler. Image: RCBS

ought to sort your brass by caliber first. When you vibrate .45 ACP, .40 S&W, 9mm, .380 ACP and .32 ACP cartridges together with the dry tumbling media, the smaller cases will invariably get stuck inside the larger ones. The pieces of walnut or corn cob media act like wedges and make it near impossible to separate the cases. If you do batches of similar calibers, you can avoid this problem.

Ultrasonic Cleaners

You can also buy an ultrasonic cleaner like this Lyman Turbo Sonic model that I use. The drawback to wet cleaning methods like ultrasonic is that you have to let your brass casings thoroughly dry. I mean bone dry, inside and out. Unless you bake it in your oven for an hour at the lowest temperature, that can take a day or so. But it will be nice and shiny!

One advantage to ultrasonic cleaning is that you don't have to pre-sort brass before cleaning. Just dump it all in and it doesn't matter if smaller cases work their way into larger ones. They'll still

This Lyman Products ultrasonic cleaner is small, but can clean hundreds of cases in minutes.

get clean and there is no gritty media that jams them together.

RELOADING PRESS

This component is required. Fortunately, it helps you complete several of the steps of reloading. Think of a reloading press like one of those old Play Doh factories. You know, the ones where you dump Play Doh in a hopper and press a big lever so it comes out like spaghetti? Like the Play Doh factory, a reloading press is just a device that uses mechanical advantage to squish things together.

A reloading press can be used to:

▷ Press a brass case against a decapping pin to push out the old primer.

▷ Press a casing into a resizing die that jams the brass back into its original dimensions.

Here's an RCBS single stage reloading press. Each pull of the handle pushes a piston up towards the hole in the top of the frame. A reloading die screws into that hole to perform the desired function. Image: RCBS

▷ Press a new primer into the now empty primer pocket.

▷ Press the casing against an expanding die that opens the mouth just a tad so you can insert a new bullet.

▷ Press the bullet down into the casing.

▷ Crimp the casing around the bullet to remove the bell from the expansion step.

You can achieve some of these steps with different equipment. For example, I often use a hand priming tool to insert new primers. But for simplicity, and the recommended minimum equipment set, we'll rely on the reloading press for all of the above steps.

What type of reloading press do you need to get started? I always recommend starting with a single stage press. Single stage means the press does one thing at a time. Using a single stage press, you'll load in batches. For example, you'll resize all your cases, then prime them all, then add powder, then seat the bullet and finally crimp all of the cases.

To perform the different steps listed above, you'll need to reconfigure it — usually by changing the reloading die. Don't know what a reloading die is? Now worries, we'll talk about that next.

RELOADING DIES

Reloading dies are simply cylinders made of steel that are used like "inserts" with your reloading press. As the interior of the reloading dies are cut specifically to match the shape of the type of cartridge, you need a set of dies for each caliber you wish to reload.

Since reloading is tactical cooking, let's use a baking analogy here. Cake decorators use an icing bag and interchangeable icing

Here's a set of pistol reloading dies from RCBS. Left to right: Decapping and resizing die, mouth expander die and seating and crimping die. Image: RCBS

tips to make different patterns on, oh, say, yellow cakes with Waldorf icing. Yum! Anyway, the icing bag is like a reloading press — squeeze it and icing comes out. Those little tips of different shapes are like reloading dies — each one fits on the bag and serves a slightly different purpose. Make sense sorta?

The reloading die screws into the reloading press. The press is then used to jam the cartridge case into the reloading die to perform the specific function of that die. For example, there are three types of dies in most pistol caliber reloading die sets.

Decapping and Resizing Die

This die does two things in one step. A steel rod right in the center goes through the open mouth of your cartridge brass and pushes out the old blown up primer.

The die itself is shaped exactly like the outside of your cartridge brass and the diameter of the die hole is the exact dimension specified for that caliber cartridge diameter. It "pushes" the brass cartridge back to the proper diameter so it will easily fit in the chamber of your gun. Remember earlier when we talked about how cartridge cases expand a little when you fire them?

Expanding Die

The resizing die reshapes the whole cartridge case back into a proper sized tube. But wait! We're going to have to stick a new bullet in there at some point, right? Will it fit? That's where the expanding die steps in. This one simply opens the very end of the open mouth of the cartridge case so you can fit a new bullet in there.

Seating and Crimping Die

This is another die that accomplishes two tasks. First, it pushes the bullet down into the case to the proper depth, based on how you adjust it. At the same time, it presses the case mouth inwards to remove the mouth expansion created during the expansion step. Perfect adjustment is critical here as you are pushing a bullet into place and pressing against it at the same time. Some pistol die sets, like Lee Deluxe Pistol Die Sets, have four dies. These simply separate the seating and crimping functions into two separate dies. Treating seating and crimping as separate operations can be a little more forgiving.

You'll need a set of dies for each caliber you wish to reload. You'll also need a shell

The metal disk holding the base of this .308 cartridge case is a shell holder. It slides into place on top of the piston of this single stage reloading press.

holder for each caliber. A shell holder is a small insert for your reloading press. It slips onto the top of the piston of your reloading press and grips the rim of your cartridge case — holding it snug while you jam the case into the reloading dies. Some die sets include a shell holder and some do not, so be sure to check and order it separately if needed. You'll also need a shell holder for each caliber you want to reload. Calibers with the exact same case rim dimensions, like .38 Special and .357 Magnum, can use the same shell holder.

RELOADING BLOCKS

Reloading blocks are trays that hold your cartridges while you're working on various steps. Since you're most likely starting with a single stage reloading press, you'll be doing things in batches. For example, once you add powder to cases, you'll need a way to securely hold those cases until you're ready to seat bullets.

You can make your own by drilling proper sized holes in a piece of wood for each caliber you reload, but blocks that accommodate multiple cartridge sizes are cheap and handy. Some starter kits include a reloading block.

Reloading blocks come in handy. A universal one like
this holds all sizes of cartridges.

POWDER SCALE

A scale is an absolute necessity. Charging cartridges with either too little or too much powder is dangerous!

Either a mechanical or electronic scale is used to make sure your powder dispenser is releasing the desired amount each time. Most starter kits include a scale or you can buy one separately.

Beam Scales

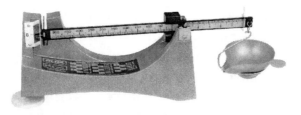

If you're ancient like me, you might remember scales like this from grade
school chemistry class. This one is an RCBS Beam scale designed specif-
ically for reloading as it weighs in grain measurements. It's hard to go
wrong with a scale like this — it always works. Image: RCBS

It's hard to go wrong with a good old-fashioned beam scale. It's a mechanical device, so unless you damage it, weight readings will be consistent and accurate. And the batteries never run out, because there are none!

If I ever am in doubt about the reading on my electronic scale, I double check using the beam scale. If I was only going to buy one scale, it would be this style.

Digital Scales

Digital scales are fast and easy. I've also found them to be plenty accurate. You do have to pay attention to your battery power level and be sure to "zero" your scale frequently. Most electronic scales will include a weight and instructions to re-calibrate the scale so you are sure that it's measuring correctly. It never hurts to do this frequently.

This Frankford Arsenal digital scale is inexpensive, but gets the job done.

Be sure to buy a scale built for ammunition reloading. It will have measurements in grains, or $1/7000_{th}$ of a pound increments.

POWDER DISPENSER

Your scale will verify the weight of the powder you're putting into a reloaded cartridge. Certainly, you can weight each and every charge you produce, but that would really slow down your process. If you're reloading a small number of very carefully produced rounds, this is fine. If you need to make 500 9mm cartridges for your weekend shooting activity, then you'll spend a month doing it.

A powder dispenser simply automates the process of measuring the correct amount of powder. It dispenses by volume, like a scoop, and relies on setting a volume exactly equal to the weight of the powder charge you need.

There are a couple of ways you can "dispense" powder amounts of your desired charge weight.

Scoops!

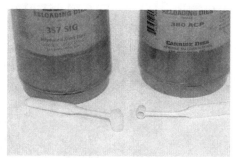

Some reloading die sets, like many from Lee Precision, include a plastic scoop that corresponds to a given weight of a certain type of powder. As each powder brand and type has different density, your scoop will

Powder scoops like these are included with Lee Precision reloading dies.

correspond to only one weight for each brand or type of powder. The idea is that you fill the scoop exactly level to the rim and that's your powder measure.

You can do this, and it's essentially free, but I don't recommend it. You don't get a lot of precision with this method and your powder charge measures are limited by the number of scoops you collect.

Powder Dispenser

To me, this little gem is well worth the money and worthy of inclusion in the most basic reloading setup. It's a hopper that holds a bunch of powder, with a lever-activated dispenser at the bottom. It operates a little bit like a soft ice cream machine, although it's a lot more precise and doesn't taste nearly as good. The key difference is that a powder measure allows a certain amount of powder to fill a measuring chamber before you dump it. So rather than a continuous flow like the ice cream machine, a specific amount is "dumped" with each lever pull. The measuring chamber is made to be almost infinitely adjustable so you can change the volume of powder dispensed.

The process of using a powder dispenser is simple. Dispense a charge. Weigh it with your scale. Adjust the dispenser to increase or decrease the amount of powder it just dumped. Repeat this process until your dispenser is dumping the exact weight that you want each time. You'll have to weigh and adjust a few times, but once you get it set, you can dispense hundreds of charges very quickly. Most dispensers have a cone-shaped bottom so you just hold the empty cartridge case against the dispenser, pull the lever and it dumps the powder directly into your cartridge case.

This powder dispenser tom RCBS has a hopper to hold powder. The cylinder in the middle has an adjustable meter that allows you to dump a specific amount of powder with each pull of the handle. Image: RCBS

CALIPERS

While not included in most starter kits, I think calipers are a must-have item. Available in analog dial or digital, a caliper accurately measures things. Sounds technical when you say it that way, right?

The most important measurement you'll need to worry about is the overall cartridge length. It's critical to make sure that your bullets are seated enough to feed reliably, but not so much that you reduce interior case volume and risk dangerous over pressure. A reloading manual will tell you exactly how deep to seat each caliber and specific bullet type. We'll talk a lot more about seating depth and overpressure in the *Bullet Seating* chapter, so don't worry if that does not make a lot of sense yet.

Calipers are also handy for checking diameter of your cases, but generally, your dies will ensure that cases are sized to the right width.

If you are going to reload bottleneck rifle cartridges, you'll also need calipers to make sure that your resized cases are the proper

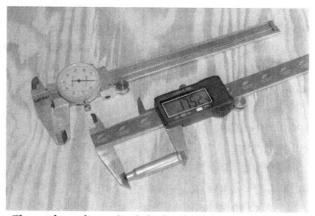

The analog calipers (top) don't rely on battery power like the digital set (bottom) but are harder to read.

length before you start to seat bullets. They tend to stretch a bit when you fire and resize them.

I have both digital and analog calipers and have found both to be more or less equally accurate and reliable. Of course, you have to worry about changing batteries with the digital type, but they're a lot easier to read. With analog calipers, you have to look at both the slide and dial to get the entire reading in inches, tenths, hundredths and thousandths.

RELOADING MANUAL

Do not reload ammunition, ever, without a reloading manual. Think of this as the cookbook full of recipes for each caliber, powder type, primer type and bullet type and weight. Reloading component and equipment companies like Hornady, Lyman, Speer, Barnes, Nosler, Sierra and Lee all publish books with detailed recipe information. Always, always, always stick within published guidelines for your reloads!

You can safely start with a single reloading manual, and many starter kits include one. Given the almost infinite number of com-

You'll want several reloading manuals like these when you start to reloading multiple calibers. They all feature different combinations of projectiles and powders.

binations of calibers, powders, primers and bullets, you'll want to add more manuals to your collection before too long.

OPTIONAL STUFF (THAT YOU REALLY SHOULD BUY)

Even if you're just planning to reload pistol cartridges, there are some pieces of equipment that can save you a lot of time and aggravation. You don't need them to start, but may want to add them to your short-term wish list. These accessories are also great gift ideas for Mother's Day, Father's Day, birthdays, Flag day, Tuesdays and any other day you might want to celebrate.

AMMO BOXES

While not technically required gear right off the bat, it's really nice to build up a collection of plastic ammo boxes.

Some people recycle cardboard factory ammo boxes, but that makes me nervous. I don't like the idea of having the "wrong" label on a box of ammunition.

Ammo boxes have a couple of benefits. Most come with lots of stickers so your can easily label your exact load data on the box. They also safely store your ammo, so you don't have to worry about primers getting bonked and set off. Last, it's easy to keep track of quantity as boxes come in 10, 20, 50 and 100 round versions.

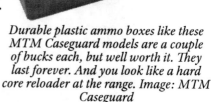

Durable plastic ammo boxes like these MTM Caseguard models are a couple of bucks each, but well worth it. They last forever. And you look like a hard core reloader at the range. Image: MTM Caseguard

You don't need them day one, but when you have a few dollars to spare, start building your collection. You'll be glad you did.

HAND PRIMING TOOL

This is a tough one to leave off the basic equipment list. But you don't technically need it, assuming the reloading press you are buying has a primer seating function. What's a primer seating function you ask? That just refers to the process of jamming a new primer into the base of your cartridge. It take a bit of pressure, hence the need for a tool of some sort.

The thought process behind hand priming tools is that you can easily, and cheaply, prime hundreds and hundreds of cartridge cases per hour. Better yet, you can do this from the comfort

With a hand priming tool like this, you empty a box of 100 primers into the tray, shake it a bit to orient them all face-up and start priming. Each squeeze of the handle pushes a primer into place. You'll need a specific shell holder for each caliber to hold the case steady while inserting primers. Image: RCBS

of, well, just about anywhere. "Hand priming tool" is a literal descriptor and most of them are small, light and portable. Want to camp out in the family room? No problem, bring a box of cases, your priming tool and an empty box for your completed cases.

Since you're using hand pressure to push primers into place, you'll want to buy a hand tool that operates smoothly and has a comfortable grip. Inserting a hundred primers won't tire your hand muscles, but you'll quickly see the value of an ergonomic priming tool when doing a thousand at a time.

One other thing to be aware of: some hand priming tools use the same shell holders that your reloading press uses. Others require special shell holders. Be sure to check to see if you need shell holders.

BULLET PULLER

Hey, with any new endeavor, you're going to mess up now and then right? An inertia bullet puller is like a hollow hammer. You unscrew a cap on one end, insert a cartridge into a special holding

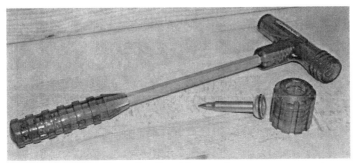

An impact bullet puller like this one allows you to correct mistakes. Insert the cartridge (like this messed up .223) into the end, screw on the retaining cap, and smack it against a hard surface like a hammer.

ring, screw the cap back on, and whack it on the floor — hard! This action knocks the bullet and powder out of the case so you can start over. As the bullet puller body is hollow, it even catches the bullet and powder so you can reuse both.

I know. Since you're reading this book, the odds of you ever making a mistake are slimmer than Nancy Pelosi's chances of becoming President of the NRA, but it's good to have. Just in case.

But seriously, having the option to "undo" a cartridge and start over will not just save you money. More importantly, it will remove temptation to let a potential mistake slide. Not sure about that last powder charge? Better safe than sorry — use your bullet puller to start over. All it costs you is a couple of minutes.

RIFLE AMMUNITION RELOADING EQUIPMENT

If you want to reload bottleneck rifle ammunition like .223 Remington, .30-30 or .308, then you'll need a couple of extras.

The two primary differences in rifle cartridge reloading relate to the fact that you need to lubricate cases before resizing and that cases stretch during resizing, so they need to be trimmed.

CASE LUBE KIT

Left to right: lubrication pad, spray on case lube and dry mica.

Unlike most pistol cartridges, which don't require lubrication prior to resizing, rifle cases do. We'll explain the reasons why in the *Resizing the Brass* chapter. For now, just trust me — you'll need a way to lubricate your brass cartridge cases.

There are a couple of approaches to case lubrication.

First is the spray-on method. As you can probably guess, this involves an aerosol or pump spray bottle. You simply lay your brass out on a tray or reloading block and spray the lubricant on the exterior of your cartridge cases. The best part of this method? No equipment required!

Second is the lubrication pad. If you're ancient like me, you might remember stamp pads. If you're not ancient, a stamp pad is a flat box with a sponge-like material inside. You soaked the interior with ink so you could press a stamp onto the pad, then stamp things like "PAID!" on bills and such. A lubrication pad works on the same principle. It's just a very flat plastic box with a pad material inside. You dampen the pad with a special lubricant and roll cartridge cases around on the pad until they're all greased up.

Even if you choose the spray on method, you'll probably want a lubrication pad. It's the tried and true fail-safe method for finicky calibers like .223 Remington.

CASE TRIMMER

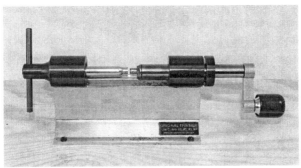

This hand-operated case trimmer shaves the mouth end of a stretched case to bring it back to proper length.

When you resize rifle cartridge brass, it will stretch a little each time you reload it. So you'll need to invest in a simple device that trims excess brass from the mouth of the case. The classic hand-operated choice is the Forster Case Trimmer.

The idea for almost all types of case trimmers is simple. It's a lathe-type tool, either hand-operated or electric. You fasten the brass cartridge case on the rim end and a rotating blade trims off the excess brass from the open neck of the cartridge.

For low volumes, a hand operated version like the Forster is just fine. If you have to do more than a hundred cases with a hand model though, you'll wish you were putting your tongue on a hot rifle barrel instead. It gets tiring and tedious with high volume.

If you know you're going to be reloading a lot of rifle cartridges, then you may want to invest in an electric case trimmer right off the bat.

CHAMFER AND DEBURRING TOOL

When you trim brass with your case trimmer, it will leave rough edges inside and outside of the case mouth from all that metal cutting.

You can smooth out the edges with a simple hand tool that performs two functions. The deburring blades take the rough edges off the outside of the newly trimmed case mouth. This also helps the cartridge fit into your dies properly. The chamfer blade works on the inside

All you really need is a simple hand tool like this RCBS model. The left side chamfers (bevels) the inside of the case mouth for easier bullet seating and the right side deburrs (smooths out) the exterior of the case mouth. Image: RCBS

of the open case mouth. Not only does it smooth the rough edges of the cut brass, it creates a very slight bevel that allows bullets to seat smoothly.

Like the case trimmers, you can get hand tools or electric tools for high volume. Deburring and chamfering doesn't take a lot of work, so a hand tool will allow you to quickly and easily process a fairly large volume of cases. If you're going to reload many hundreds, or thousands, of rifle cartridges at a time, you might want to invest in an electric case prep station that uses electronic motors for deburring and chamfering. These machines usually include additional attachments for other functions like cleaning primer pockets.

RELOADING STARTER KITS

Most reloading equipment vendors offer starter kits. In my view, this is the way to go if you're just getting started.

You'll get a substantial discount for buying a complete set from one manufacturer rather than piecemeal components. It's cheaper for the manufacturer to bundle a number of parts together and it's in their best interest to get your hooked on their brand as you'll almost certainly buy more accessories and goodies over time.

A starter kit usually includes the following, but be sure to check the contents of the one you buy to make sure it has everything you want.

- ▷ Single stage reloading press

- ▷ Scale

- ▷ Powder dispenser

- ▷ Powder funnel

- ▷ Priming tool (Either integrated with the reloading press or separate)

- ▷ Reloading tray

- ▷ Chamfer / deburring tool

- ▷ Reloading manual or guide

*This RCBS Turret Deluxe Reloading Kit has everything you
need except the caliber-specific die set. Image: RCBS*

You'll almost certainly need to purchase your reloading die set
and shell holder separately as there are so many. It just doesn't
make sense to create separate kits for various calibers. You might
also find that some starter kits include a hand-operated case trimmer. This is a big plus if you plan to start with reloading rifle
calibers.

I recommend sticking with a name brand reloading equipment
maker for your starter kit. RCBS, Hornady, Redding and Lyman
and Lee Precision all make excellent starter sets with different
combinations of gear. It's hard to go wrong with any of these.

Chapter Five

BRASS PREPARATION AND CLEANING

I named this chapter *Brass Preparation* instead of *Brass Cleaning* as there are really a few different steps involved — filtering, sorting and finally cleaning.

> *When sorting and cleaning brass, I like to use latex gloves. At risk of being called a sissy, I find that this really helps keep your hands clean, but more importantly, it minimizes exposure to dangerous stuff that comes from shooting range floors and spent cartridges — lead residue. Also, a properly fitting pair of disposable latex gloves makes handling and separating small pieces of brass a little easier as the gloves are "grippier" than your fingers. You can find them in large quantities dirt cheap at wholesale clubs like Sam's or CostCo.*

Before you think about cleaning, it's a great idea to filter, sort and kill the Berdans! Don't know what a Berdan is? Stay tuned for a minute and we'll clear that up.

FILTERING BRASS

Filtering for me means separating "real" brass from "fake" brass. By fake, I mean unusable for reloading purposes. For example, some budget ammunition uses aluminum cartridge cases. There's nothing wrong with that as the whole idea is to make practice ammo more affordable by using non-reloadable materials for the case. The ammo manufacturer certainly doesn't make money when you reload their nice brass cartridge cases. Other ammunition, including a number of imported brands, use steel cases for the same reason. By the time you read this book, you might even start seeing a few polymer cases at your range. Yes, plastic!

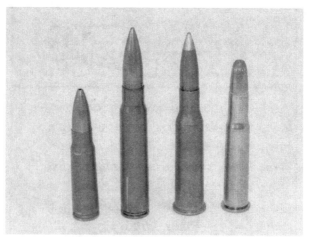

Only the cartridge on the far right is reloadable, as it's made from brass. The others are easy to spot as they are either dull grey, green or copper colored. You also might encounter shiny silver cartridges. These are reloadable too as they are nickel coated brass.

The only reason I mention aluminum, steel and polymer cases is that you can't reload them! Well, OK, technically you can reload some of them, like steel cases, once or twice, but it doesn't work very well because they are brittle and crack easily. My recommendation? Send them to the trash! Brass is a flexible metal, so you can mash it back into shape and reload it. Usually, you can reload a brass cartridge between five and ten times. Not too shabby, right?

INSPECTING BRASS

Once you've narrowed down your brass to cases actually made of brass, you'll need to inspect them for damage and wear.

For any cases, rifle or pistol, if you see any indication of wear or damage, throw them away! Reloading a damaged case is not worth the risk. You really, really don't want a case to rupture when you fire it.

Look for obvious cracks or splits. Also look for stretch marks. Although rare, cases that are stretching too far when fired may indicate problems with your gun. If you notice ejected cartridge cases from your gun coming out with obvious damage, have a gunsmith check over your firearm.

If a case is badly dented, toss it.

Look at the case mouths for small cracks or splits. These can be easy to miss.

Although you will get to this step later, you also want to be on the lookout for enlarged primer pockets. One sign you might see during the inspection stage are burn marks on the bottom of the case resulting from gas escaping through the primer pocket. Later in the reloading process, when inserting new primers, if you notice one goes in too easily, that might be a sign of a worn primer pocket. Throw that case away too!

This is also a good time to look for signs that your gun and or reloads are problematic.

Check the base of your cartridge cases. Are the letters in the case head stamp squashed flat or deformed? That may indicate problems. Is the spent primer pierced all the way through? That might also indicate trouble with your gun or cartridges.

If you see abnormal signs, stop and get your gun checked out. Also check your reloads to make sure you're operating in a safe range.

SORTING BRASS

I can't make up my mind whether I prefer cleaning brass with a dry tumbler, an ultrasonic cleaner or a wet stainless steel pin tumbler. I guess I like to tinker and play, so I tend to switch back and forth between methods based on tidal charts, the Farmers Almanac and whether Brad Pitt has a beard or not.

You have to sort your brass at least by caliber at some point as you don't want to be trying to seat 9mm bullets in a .223 Remington cartridge case. Most of the time, I sort my brass by caliber before cleaning. I've become a habitual Housewares aisle shopper at my local Wal-Mart because I buy plastic tubs by the metric ton. When you get obsessed like I am, you'll want empty bins for each caliber you reload for both dirty and clean brass. So, for example, 9mm brass requires two tubs — one for dirty and the other for clean.

Plastic containers like these are available at any discount store and are handy for sorting different calibers of brass.

Although it's a messy process, and your hands will get filthy, there's a good reason to sort your brass before cleaning, especially if you use a dry tumbler. As we touched on in the *Basic Equipment Requirements* chapter, small caliber brass can get jammed inside larger caliber brass when dry tumbling. If you load your tumbler with all the same caliber, you don't have this problem!

BOXER VS. BERDAN PRIMERS

There is one more "sorting and filtering" chore. Fortunately this step can be done after the brass is cleaned.

You need to spot any cartridge cases that use Berdan primers. Since you're about to ask what on earth a Berdan primer is, let's take a quick diversion. It's an important one, though, as running a Berdan primer through your resizing and recapping die will break the pin. This isn't a huge tragedy, but will force you to call the die manufacturer and order spare parts. Waiting on the mail really slows down your reloading speed. Trust me on this, I know.

Shortly after the invention of the rock, a couple of smart guys started to experiment with different ways to ignite ammunition cartridges. Fortunately they were on different continents, else there might have been a rumble.

Berdan Primers

Hiram Berdan, an inventor in New York, patented his priming idea in 1866. With the Berdan system, the primer is still inserted into the center of the cartridge base. The cartridge case itself has a shaped "anvil" or in simpler terms, a "pointy thing" in the center of the base. This is surrounded by two or three off-center holes that connect the primer pocket to the interior of the case. When the primer is struck by the firing pin, it presses up against the anvil portion of the case and blows up. Flame shoots through the multiple holes and ignites the propellant.

Boxer Primers

At almost exactly the same time, Colonel Edward Mounier Boxer developed a similar system while working with the Royal Arsenal at Woolwich, England. Boxer's design had the anvil as a portion of the primer itself. So when the firing pin hits the base of the primer, it pushes the base of the primer against the anvil piece of the primer, causing a small explosion. The flame travels through a single, larger hole right in the center of the cartridge case to ignite the propellant.

Both systems work just fine. The Berdan primers are easier to manufacture because they don't have a separate anvil piece. However, they're very difficult to reload, because it's hard to remove the spent primer. The Boxer primers are more complex to manufacture, but much easier to reload.

All this trivia is good and nice, but when it comes to learning how to make more 9mm ammunition for your range outings, who cares?

You do! And here's why. A Berdan cartridge case has two, and

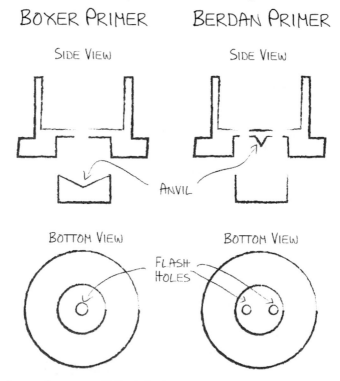

sometimes three small flash holes in the bottom of the cartridge. And none of them are in the center. Your decapping die has a single "pin" that is designed to push straight down through the center of a cartridge case. This is intended to push out a Boxer primer, which uses a larger single hole in the dead center of the cartridge case. When you put a Berdan case through your die, the decapping pin pushes down, under lots of pressure, straight into a piece of hard brass with no hole! And it bends or breaks! You can easily fix the pin, but it's a giant pain in the butt.

It's important to find the Berdan cases before you start resizing cases. I recommend smashing them with a pair of pliers and throwing them away, so they don't get mixed back in to your reusable Boxer-primed brass.

Don't panic about the thought of looking carefully through the mouth of each and every brass cartridge. Berdan primers are not all that common, and fortunately they are limited to (mostly) overseas manufacturers. You'll quickly learn which brands use Berdan primers so you can just look at the head stamp on the bottom to identify them.

HOW TO CLEAN YOUR BRASS

It's time to clean the brass! In my view, this is the part of reloading that's the biggest headache. It's messy and dirty, and not as gratifying as producing beautiful cartridges. But it's a necessary step, so let's get to it. I'll try to point out how to make it as painless as possible along the way.

Earlier in the book, we covered the most important "pre-step" of reloading — hoarding brass like it's made of Brown Sugar Cinnamon Pop Tarts. Assuming you've been doing that, it's time to clean it. The goal of cleaning is partly cosmetic, but the real goal is to remove mud, powder residue, lead and whatever other filth that might be on your fired brass. This dirt and grime will gunk up your reloading dies and/or cause feeding problems in your gun. Other than that, there is no "technical" need to make your used brass bright and shiny again. There's nothing wrong with being proud of your reloaded ammunition, so we're going to talk about how to make it safe AND beautiful. Why shouldn't your reloads be the envy of the range?

Given the "beautiful" requirement, we're going to dispense with the backwoods method of cleaning brass — shaking it in a bucket with some Tide or perhaps a mixture of dish detergent, vinegar, and salt. This will make it safe, but not all that great looking.

Let's focus on three primary methods of brass cleaning — dry tumbling, ultrasonic cleaning and wet tumbling.

Dry Tumbling

Otherwise known as tumbling, the dry method involves vibrating or tumbling the spent brass in a mixture of what reloaders call "media." As tempting as it is to make a wisecrack about the potential uses of mainstream "media" for things like scrubbing dirt, I'll refrain. Reloading media is the material that goes in the tumbler with your brass. Media can be made of natural or syn-

Here's a dry tumbler (actually it vibrates) from RCBS. Image: RCBS

thetic materials. Natural materials include ground walnut shells and ground corn cob. Some media is impregnated with polish to help your brass come out even cleaner.

Most dry tumblers actually vibrate, although a few models use a rotating drum like those home rock polishers that were so popular back in the day. A large plastic bowl with a clamped on lid is mounted on an electric motor that vibrates the bowl and its contents. You fill the bowl with both media and dirty brass, clamp the lid on, and let it run. It hums. It shakes. It causes neighbors to wonder if a 3.2 scale earthquake is in progress. After anywhere from thirty minutes to a couple of hours, depending on the condition of the dirty brass, you turn it off.

The dirt from your brass needs to go somewhere. Generally, it rubs off from your brass onto the media material itself. That new and pretty media very quickly turns black and icky from all the range gunk. Not only is this unattractive and gross, it reduces cleaning effectiveness of the media. It's kind of like trying to clean a floor with a filthy mop — you just end up moving dirt around. If you want to make your media last longer, and get cleaner brass in the process, tear a couple of used dryer sheets (like Bounce) into the tumbler. The sheets will attract most of the dirt, keeping your media fresh for many more uses.

See how these used dryer sheets are attracting the dirt?

After your brass is clean enough, you need to separate the media from the clean brass. Some tumblers have a built in filter that allows the media to be drained out while the machine is running. If yours doesn't, you can pick up a case media sifter to speed the process.

Whatever the method for separating your cleaned brass from the media, you need to be sure that all cases are completely empty of media. This can be tricky in rifle cases with small necks like the .223 Remington. Sometimes, pieces of media get stuck inside the case and don't want to come out.

This RCBS rotary media separator couldn't be easier to use. Dump the whole mess, media and brass, into the hopper, close the lid and crank away. Soon, the cage area will have only brass and the media will have fallen to the bottom container for reuse. Image: RCBS

I use the vibration of the tumbler itself to shake loose stuck media in small-mouth cases like .223 Remington. Scoop a few cases out of the tumbler and hold them upside down while pressed against the side or center post of the tumbler while it's on. The vibration quickly knocks all loose pieces out. For pistol cases and rifle cases with larger mouths, this is rarely necessary.

I recommend spending a few bucks and buying media designed for brass cleaning when you're just starting out. Lyman Products make a range of tumbling media products. Some even have polish impregnated to shine up your brass cases. The reason I recommend starting with a packaged product is consistency of size of the media particles. If they're too small, they can get stuck in primer pockets and flash holes. If they are to large, they get stuck in the case bodies. With manufactured brass tumbling media, you rarely have to worry about these things.

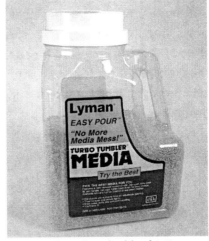

Pre-packaged media like this Lyman product will help you keep things simple. You'll get a lot of cleanings from this tub, as the media is reusable.

As you gain experience, and perhaps a desire to save a few dollars, you can find your own tumbling media. Pet supply and feed stores often sell crushed walnut shells or ground corn cobs for pet bedding. You can get large quantities cheap. Before you have a truckload delivered, try some and make sure the size works well for you.

When dry tumbling, I prefer to clean the brass while the spent primers are still in place. This prevents media from getting stuck in primer pockets.

Ultrasonic Cleaning

You can also use an ultrasonic cleaner to clean your brass to like-new condition. Most reloading equipment manufacturers offer an ultrasonic cleaner as well as cleaning solvents for both brass and steel products. Yes, once you invest in an ultrasonic cleaner, you can use it to clean gun parts too! Just be sure to use the right solution for brass and steel cleaning. Some ultrasonic cleaners even have an integrated heater, which helps the cleaning process even more.

One of the nice benefits of using an ultrasonic cleaner is that you don't have to sort the brass by caliber before cleaning. Since the cleaning "media" is liquid, cases won't get jammed inside of each other. So you can just clean everything, then sort-

This Lyman ultrasonic cleaner will do hundreds of cases in minutes.

ing the clean brass by caliber will be a little easier. Your choice.

The cleaning process couldn't be easier. Fill the unit to the line with water. Add the right amount of cleaning solvent. Lower the basket of dirty brass into the mixture. Cover and run for just a few minutes. Yes, minutes. My Lyman TurboSonic unit cleans the dirtiest, nastiest range brass in less than five minutes.

When using an ultrasonic cleaner, I like to use a general purpose recapping die to remove spent primers first. These dies don't do any resizing, so it doesn't matter that the brass is dirty. With the primer removed, an ultrasonic cleaner will do a great job of cleaning the primer pockets and flash holes. With the primer removed, wet cases also dry faster.

The "gotcha" is that your brass finishes the cleaning process soaking wet, so it needs to be dried. You can spread it out on a towel in the sun. If you're feeling brave, you can put it on a cookie sheet in your oven at the lowest temperature for a bit. Do this at your own risk as it could easily offend the household chef! And even though the brass is technically clean, I, for one, am not all that crazy about cooking formerly lead-infused cartridge casings in the same oven that makes my food. Call me crazy.

There's always the old-school way to dry wet brass... throw them on a towel for a day or so, shuffling occasionally.

I think the best solution is to get yourself a food dehydrator. To over-simplify, this is a small, low temperature oven with lots of shelves. Sprinkle wet brass on each of the shelves and let it run. At only 150 degrees or so, it won't get hot enough to damage your brass but will dry it thoroughly and relatively quickly.

Wet Tumbling

This method is a hybrid between dry tumbling and ultrasonic. While no magical sound waves are involved, it tumbles with liquid.

Obviously, using a corn cob or walnut shell tumbling media would make a soggy mess. The wet tumbling method uses small stainless steel pins for the media. The stainless pins are or course reusable and they last forever.

You will need a special wet tumbler for this method — the dry tumblers are not designed to hold liquid! Most wet tumblers are a rotary style. You fill a watertight drum with brass, stainless steel pins water and a detergent, seal it up, and place it on a motor that rotates the drum.

Wet tumblers rotate a waterproof tub in a circular motion.
Image: RCBS.

These machines do a wonderful job of cleaning the nastiest of brass. The stainless pins are small enough to get inside of the primer pockets and flash holes, so your cartridge cases will be shiny inside and out.

Since it's a wet method, you will need to thoroughly dry your brass just as you would with the ultrasonic cleaning method.

Which Method Should You Use?

We've talked about three different methods for cleaning your brass. The bad news is that's confusing. Which do you use? The good news is that you can pick the best method for you based on what you are trying to achieve.

Here are my opinions on the matter: If you're just getting started, it's hard to go wrong with a dry tumbler. They're inexpensive and clean any type of brass. And they do a great job. You'll need to buy media periodically, but that's not particularly expensive. You also won't have to worry about drying brass. As a new reloader, you don't want to introduce the variable of tiny amounts of water buried in the depths of your cartridge cases.

When you start to get the hang of reloading, add either an ultrasonic or wet tumbler depending on your volume. If you're serious about cleaning a lot of brass, a wet tumbler is the way to go. It's relatively fast and the media lasts forever.

Just as with most of my other reloading equipment, I find that I still use multiple methods — they're not mutually exclusive. If I come home from the range with a pile of mixed brass, and I don't have a sense of urgency to reload it, I'll dump it in the ultrasonic cleaner to get it clean, then spread it out on a towel for a couple of days to let it dry. If I picked up one caliber, or if the brass is already sorted, I find myself using the dry tumbler. I think it does a better overall job of making the brass clean and shiny than an ultrasonic, and I don't have to let it dry.

Chapter Six

DECAPPING THE CARTRIDGE CASE

Before you can begin creating a new cartridge from used up pieces and parts, there is one more step to complete — decapping the fired cartridge casing.

Decap simply means removing the fired primer by pushing it out of its pocket. Why there's a fancy word for it, I have no idea.

In the previous chapter, we talked about the two types of primers in use today - Boxer and Berdan. While it's technically possible to remove a Berdan primer, it's a hassle and beyond the scope of this book. Plus, the vast majority of cartridges you will encounter use Boxer primers. The good news? Boxer primers are really easy to remove. Most of the time, removing the primer is a "freebie" part of the process of resizing the cartridge case.

Most resizing dies, like the .40 S&W on the left and .223 Remington on the right, have a decapping rod included.

As the die resizes the case, the decapping pin goes through the case mouth and pushes its pin through the flash hole, thereby pushing the primer out of the case.

This .308 case will be "decapped" as soon as it is pressed into this general purpose decapping die.

So the simplest method of decapping is not really an extra step at all as it happens automatically during resizing.

However, there are times when you may choose to remove the primer as a separate operation from resizing the cartridge case. You may use an ultrasonic or wet tumbling cleaning method and want to make sure that the insides of the primer pockets are thoroughly cleaned before reloading.

No worries! You can use a general purpose decapping die. A decapping die looks like a resizing die, and has a decapping pin in the center. The difference is that the die body is really wide and will not touch the exterior of the cartridge case. All it does is push the primer out. There is no need to lubricate cases and the operation is fast and easy. Just insert the shell holder for the caliber you're decapping in the reloading press, screw in the decapping die and go to work.

You'll be able to adjust the spindle and pin of the decapping die to set the distance that it extends from the bottom of the die. As a general rule, only extend it just far enough to knock the primer out. The more your extend it, the less the spindle is supported by the die, and the more likely you are to bend or break the decapping pin.

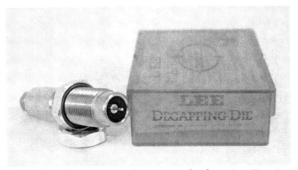

Here's an inexpensive decapping die from Lee Precision. Notice how wide the body is so it doesn't interfere with the cartridge case itself.

Chapter Seven

Resizing the Brass

Every time you fire a cartridge, lots of violent things happen inside the chamber of your gun.

The primer ignition sets flame to the propellant, which then begins to burn at an obscenely fast rate. It doesn't technically explode, but it burns so fast you might think it's exploding.

As the propellant burns, the chemical reaction creates high pressure gas, which has to go somewhere — fast. This swelling gas cloud inside your cartridge does two things.

First, it expands the brass cartridge case until it's pressing against the inside walls of the gun's chamber. Both rifle and handgun cartridges expand sideways against the wall of the chamber. The case literally increases in diameter and circumference. In the case of bottleneck rifle cartridges, the case expands lengthwise also. The shoulder of the case (the section where the case decreases in diameter) pushes forward against the chamber. All this expansion seals the cartridge case in the chamber and prevents the rapidly expanding hot gas from leaking out backwards towards you.

Next, the hot gas pushes the projectile hard enough to overcome the friction of the cartridge case mouth and launch it down the gun barrel. As the bullet leaves the cartridge, and the pressure starts to drop. This is because the available space increases as the bullet travels down the barrel. As pressure and temperature begin to drop, the brass cartridge case starts to shrink back closer to its original size — but not all the way.

65

A fired cartridge case will almost always be a little larger than an identical, but unfired, one. Also, the cartridge case mouth will be opened up a bit as a bullet that was comfortably seated there has just been violently ejected.

All of this happens in a split second, but has a lasting impact. It's the reason that, when reloading your own ammunition, you need to resize the brass cartridge case. While resizing the cartridge case rarely compresses it to its original size, it will crush it back within cartridge dimension standards, allowing it to chamber in any gun of the proper caliber.

RESIZING DIES

A resizing die is simply a carefully shaped hunk of metal that is used to "press" the empty cartridge case back to standardized dimensions. The brass cartridge case is forced into the interior of the die with a reloading press. The internal shape of the resizing die presses the brass back into the proper dimensions.

Think of this process kind of like making a hamburger. You take a misshapen pile of ground beef, and using pressure from the outside, you shape it into the desired form. With fired brass, you take a cartridge case that has contained a massive conflagration, and therefore expanded in size, and press it back into shape. Unlike the hamburger, brass is hard, and tastes lousy, hence the need for a steel reloading die and a reloading press to apply the necessary amount of pressure.

Brass is not as easy to reshape as hamburger meat, and significantly more pressure than available with bare hands is required to reshape it to standard size. Why

Here's a cutaway view of a rifle cartridge resizing die. Note the shell-shaped cavity in the die body. The spindle pushes out the spent primer during resizing. Image: RCBS

does this matter? If you're not careful, pressing the case into a steel resizing die under great pressure can cause the case to get stuck inside of the die. Why? Unlike hamburger meat, neither brass nor steel have yummy, slippery fat grease by default. So, when resizing cartridge case brass, you need to have some type of lubrication.

Depending on the type of cartridge you're resizing, lubrication can be a separate operation, or in the case of most pistol cartridges, the die itself is "slippery enough" to meet lubrication needs. We'll address that in more detail when we talk about the specifics of resizing rifle and pistol cartridges next.

PISTOL BRASS (STRAIGHT WALL CARTRIDGES)

Resizing straight-wall pistol cartridges is really easy. By "straight wall" I simply mean that the cartridge case is shaped like a cylinder that has the same diameter from the rim of the cartridge to the mouth. Like a toilet paper roll or aluminum soda can.

Examples of straight wall cartridges, left to right: 9mm. .40 S&W, .45 ACP, .38 Special, .357 Magnum and .44 Magnum.

Not all pistol cartridge cases are like this. A great example of an exception is the .357 Sig, which is shaped more like an old Coke bottle — it narrows as you get closer to the case mouth. In these rare cases, you need to resize as you would a bottleneck rifle cartridge. We'll get to that in a minute.

Even though most pistol cartridges have straight walls and resizing is minimal, lubrication is still required. A clever reloading engineer figured out how to gain a lubrication effect by using a material other than steel in the reloading die. As it turned out, carbide is a little more slick than standard steel. If you could make a reloading die out of carbide, then additional lubrication would not be required.

Although not as common, there are bottleneck pistol cartridges, like these .357 Sigs.

The only problem with using carbide is that, while it's plenty hard, it's also brittle. This means it's very difficult to make a bottleneck cartridge shaped die entirely out of carbide. For straight-walled cartridges, all you really need is a carbide ring at the bottom — there's no need to make the whole die out of Carbide. As the Carbide ring "insert" in the bottom of the steel reloading die moves over the cartridge case, it resizes as it goes.

This .40 S&W case is about to be resized and decapped in one operation. The case is set in a shell holder and the die is adjusted to resize and push out the old primer.

If you buy a carbide die set, you don't need to do any special lubrication for straight walled pistol cases. Just so you know, some die manufacturers are starting to find new materials that accomplish the same thing as carbide. For example, Hornady uses a titanium nitride finish that's even harder than carbide and requires no lubrication. Just be sure the pistol dies you purchase have a similar feature, whether it's made of carbide or something similar. It will save you a lot of hassle.

Straight-Walled Cartridge Resizing Steps

Here are the basic steps to resize a straight-walled handgun cartridge.

▷ Attach the proper shell holder for the caliber you are resizing on the piston of your reloading press.

▷ Screw the proper resizing die into the top of the press.

▷ Raise the piston, with shell holder installed, all the way up as far as it will travel.

▷ Continue to screw in the resizing die until it just touches the top of the shell holder. This ensures that your case will be resized as close to the base as possible.

▷ Tighten the locking ring on the resizing die.

▷ Lower the piston of the reloading press.

▷ Now, you may need to adjust the "depth" of the decapping spindle and pin. The decapping pin should extend about ⅛ inch below the bottom of the resizing die. You want it to extend low enough to push a primer completely out of a cartridge case, but not more than you need.

▷ Insert a cartridge case into the shell holder.

▷ Lower the handle on your press. This will raise the piston, with the shell holder and casing, into the resizing die. Make sure the piston travels as far as it will go, then lower the case back out of the resizing die.

▷ Did it remove the primer? Great! You're all set. Continue resizing your cases. If the primer didn't come all the way out, you may need to adjust the depth of the decapping pin.

If you use a carbide resizing die, you don't need to lubricate your cases before resizing. However, if you spray some lubricant, like Hornady One Shot onto your cases, the resizing process will be much, much easier. Just read the directions on your spray lube first. Some spray lubes need to dry thoroughly before use, or else they will be even stickier than with no lube at all!

RIFLE BRASS (BOTTLENECK CARTRIDGES)

When your cartridge case is shaped more like a WWII pin up model than a soda can, there are a lot more curves to press and shape into proper dimensions with a resizing die and press. You can't just run a Carbide ring down around the case and call it done. The neck has to be the right size and length, the shoulder (bend) has to be in the right position, and the taper of the case body has to match standard specifications.

There's one more thing to consider. At risk of getting ahead our ourselves in the process, when you squish the outside of cartridge cases towards the center, a new bullet will no longer fit into the mouth easily. For straight wall cartridges, there's a step in the process called case mouth belling, which we'll cover a little later. For most rifle cartridges, this step is completed at the same time as the case resizing — the interior of the cartridge neck is resized, but not flared outwards.

Bottleneck resizing dies have a case mouth expander ball. Mounted on the spindle that holds the decapping pin, this smooth ball or oval forces its way into the case mouth to expand it to the proper size from the inside. There's a lot going on with a rifle cartridge resizing — you're pressing brass inwards, downwards and outwards all at the same time! This means there is even more opportunity for the brass case to get stuck in your reloading die because of that pesky "friction" thing. When you resize a piece of bottleneck rifle cartridge brass, you absolutely need to lubricate it first.

CASE LUBRICATION

While lubrication creates a couple of extra steps, there's one important thing to avoid. You do not want wet lubricant to get inside of the case. If it stays there, it can interfere with the proper ignition and burn of your powder.

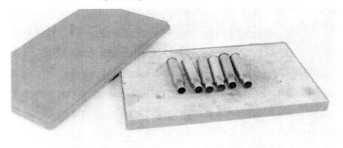

After you apply some lubricant to the pad, you can just roll cases across to prepare them for resizing.

You also have to be careful about wet lubricant left on the outside of the cartridge case. If it's left on the outside, chambering and ejection will be impacted when you try to fire it. If you remember all the conflagration that happens inside the chamber of your gun, there's a delicate balance of brass expansion in the chamber and sealing against the chamber walls until pressure and temperature drop. If lubricant is on the outside of the case, it may interfere with that process, causing malfunction or worse. I only go into this to stress the importance of removing any wet lubricant you use.

Don't use too much lubricant! If you use too much, you can even dent your case when resizing. There is a fixed amount of space inside a resizing die. If there is a big glob of lubricant, it will literally press against the side of your case until it dents. Remember high school chemistry when you learned that liquids aren't compressible? If you were sleeping or cutting class, here's a hint: the brass bends first because the liquid has to go somewhere.

When it comes to a case lubrication strategy, you have choices: You can use a "wet" lube, like this RCBS Case lube pad. The idea is to apply a little RCBS lube to the sponge-like pad and roll your brass on it before resizing. You can also use a wet spray, like RCBS Case Slick. That comes in a pump spray bottle which makes it easy to mist the lubricant over your cases. These types of "wet" lubrication approaches work great. You have to work pretty hard to get a stuck case in your resizing die if you properly "wet lube" your brass.

To remove the lubricant after resizing, you can simply wipe off the cartridge casings with a (relatively) clean rag. It doesn't have to be perfect — you just want the excess removed. If you're a perfectionist, or don't want to wipe each case individually, you can batch "re-clean" the cases with a tumbler or ultrasonic cleaner.

If you don't want to mess with the extra step of removing lubricant, you can try a "dry" lube approach. Products like Hornady's One Shot are "waxy" in nature and don't need to be removed. However, I've found them to be more sensitive to proper procedure. You need to spray on the lube, then let it dry thoroughly before resizing. If these types of dry lube aren't dry, they'll stick. Whatever approach you decide to use, read the lube instructions carefully.

One small step that makes a huge difference is brushing and/or dry lubing the interior of the case neck. Simply cleaning the gunk out of the case mouth prior to resizing reduces the resizing force significantly. If you want to the resizing step to be even more effortless, dip the open mouth into some mica powder to provide dry lubrication to the inside of the mouth. Mica powder is a dry powder lubricant, like graphite. It's available from any reloading supplier.

Bottleneck Case Resizing Steps

▷ Install the proper shell holder on your reloading press for the caliber you will be resizing.

▷ Screw the proper resizing die into the top of the press.

▷ Raise the piston, with shell holder installed, all the way up as far as it will travel.

▷ Continue to screw in the resizing die until it touches the top of the shell holder. As a general rule, you want to adjust your resizing die so that it just touches the shell holder. This ensures that your case will be resized as close to the base as possible. With a rifle cartridge resizing die, you can tighten the die down another half turn or so from when it touches the shell holder. Your reloading press will "cam over" when it encounters pressure from the shell holder. "Camming over" means that the pressure will release and you won't smash your resizing die and shell holder to bits with the mechanical force of the press. You don't want to do this with a carbide pistol cartridge die as you might crack the brittle carbide ring with too much force — always adjust those so the base of the die and shell holder are barely touching.

▷ Tighten the locking ring on the resizing die so it doesn't move.

▷ Lower the piston of the reloading press.

▷ Now, you may need to adjust the "depth" of the decapping spindle and pin. The decapping pin should extend about ⅛ inch below the bottom of the resizing die. You want it to extend low enough to push a primer completely out of a cartridge case, but not more than you need.

▷ We'll assume that you have already lubricated the cases you're going to resize using one of the methods listed above.

▷ Insert a cartridge case into the shell holder.

▷ Operate your press to push the case into the resizing die all the way and then lower it back. With a bottleneck rifle cartridge, you'll encounter a good bit of pressure, but the press will keep moving it you have lubricated the case properly. If it feels like you're hitting a hard stop, reverse the motion before you get the case stuck in the die. Then check to make sure the case is properly lubricated. Also check to make sure a Berdan primed case didn't get mixed in by mistake. You'll quickly develop a feel for the difference between heavy pressure required to reshape a case and that of a case about to get stuck in the die. If your case does get stuck, no worries, you can fix it. We'll cover that in the *Advanced Topics* chapter later.

Once the case is lubricated, the process of resizing a bottleneck rifle cartridge like this .223 Remington is the same as straight wall cartridges.

▷ Did it remove the primer? Great! You're all set. Continue resizing your cases. If the primer didn't come all the way out, you may need to adjust the depth of the decapping pin.

Using one of the methods described above, clean any excess lubricant from your newly sized cases.

One thing is sure when it comes to rifle case resizing. You'll learn by experimentation. You'll get some cases stuck, but that's just part of the learning curve. Soon, you'll be able to tell by feel when you're about to stick and you can usually avoid it.

While there are more resizing steps with rifle cartridges, the payoff for perseverance is great. Not only can you save a lot of money per cartridge, you can really tune a load to your specific gun for accuracy, power level and/or intended use.

Chapter Eight

CASE TRIMMING

When you resize bottleneck cartridges, they tend to stretch. The resizing operation presses them back into the proper diameter and forces the shoulder back into place, but in the process, the neck and mouth of the cartridge become slightly elongated.

Since all other parts of the cartridge case have been resized to proper specification, you can simply trim the excess from the end, and it's as good as new.

We're not talking a lot of extra length — the difference can be tough to see. When it comes to reloading, details are important, and that little bit of extra length can cause serious problems.

SAFETY FIRST!

If the neck of the cartridge is too long, it can extend past the chamber and into the rifled part of the barrel. If this happens, there is no room for the case neck to expand and allow the bullet to escape normally. It will fire, but the pressure will be immense — and dangerous.

At minimum, irregular case lengths will give you difficulty consistently seating and crimping bullets. Bullet seating dies place the bullet at an exact position relative to the bottom of the cartridge case, or top of the shell holder — not the top of the case.

So if every case has a different length, your bullets are going to be pressed in at all sorts of different depths.

So what to do?

No worries, trimming cases is a little tedious, but fairly easy. The first step is to make sure you have a case trimmer. I would start with a hand operated model. For accuracy of trim length and consistency, it's hard to go wrong with the Forster Case Trimmer. It's easy to adjust, will only cost you about $70 and you'll use it forever — even if you graduate to a power trimmer for larger batches.

Here's where you'll start to get valuable data from your reloading manual. Each cartridge has a standard "trim to" length specified, and your reloading manual will tell you that. For example, for .223 Remington cartridge cases, my Sierra Bullets Reloading Manual Edition Five specifies a trim-to length of 1.750 inches. That's the safe number that will ensure your cartridge fits properly into .223 Remington standard chambers.

Adjusting your hand case trimmer, like the Forster model, is a

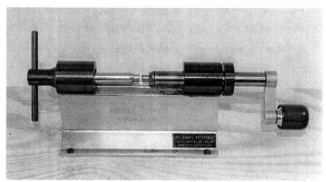

This Forster Case Trimmer locks the base of the case, left side. The spindle with cutting blade has an adjustment stop wheel on the right which specifies how far the blade can travel towards the cartridge case. It's simple and consistent.

trial and error effort. Using your calipers, you can find an empty case that is already 1.750 inches and use that as a guide, or you can start with a longer one and gradually trim and measure until you get it right.

The cutting operation is pretty simply for most hand operated trimmers. You fasten the base of the cartridge case on one side, then adjust the cutting blade position to the desired length. Most models have a "rough" adjustment to get you close, and a "fine" adjustment capability to get the thousandths-of-an-inch measurements right on target. Yes, thousandths of an inch! Remember earlier in the book when I told you reloading your own ammunition requires attention to detail? Both rough and fine adjustments will have some sort of locking screw to help keep things in position.

Once you get the blade in the right position, it's a matter of mounting the cartridge case and turning the handle to operate the cutting blade. You'll feel the pressure from cutting and see small brass shavings coming off. Careful, they're sharp and make very effective splinters! You'll know the case has been cut to the proper length when the turning motion becomes smooth as the blade is no longer cutting. Depending on how much muscle you put into it (it only takes a little) and how much needs to be trimmed, you might need anywhere from a few to dozens of turns of the handle to trim each case.

It's important to stop once in a while and measure a case to make sure your settings haven't changed.

If you get serious about reloading rifle cartridges, especially ones which you shoot in high volume, you'll want to upgrade to a power trimmer before too long. We'll talk about those in the *Advanced Equipment* chapter.

Chapter Nine

CHAMFERING AND DEBURRING

More good news! While you can do this step for straight wall pistol cartridge cases, it's not really necessary. You only really need to chamfer and deburr the case mouth after you trim it, and this generally applies to bottleneck rifle and pistol cartridges.

Unless you're doing large volumes of cases, you can do this with a simple hand tool like the one we showed in the *Basic Equipment Requirements* chapter.

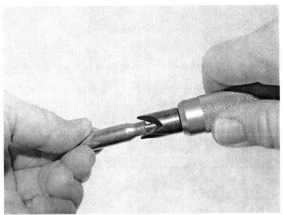

There's some serious deburring going on here! Yes, it's this easy. A couple of light twists and you're done.

To refresh your memory, deburring is the process of smoothing out rough edges left over from cutting on the outside of the case mouth.

Chamfering also smooths out rough edges from cutting, but on the inside of the case mouth. More importantly, it cuts a slight inward bevel that allows bullets to be inserted easily without scraping them all up and bending the case mouth.

The process is simple. With a hand tool, just rotate the deburring end of the tool around the case mouth for a turn or two. Flip the tool over to the chamfer blade and repeat the process. It only takes a little. Even for the chamfer bevel, a little goes a long way. You're only trying to remove that hard edge.

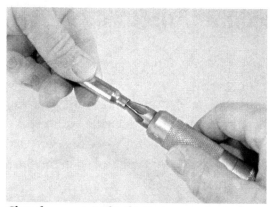

Chamfer anyone? Flip this Lyman combo tool over and the other blade chamfers the inside.

Like most operations, there are fancy tools to do this operation in bulk. We'll talk more about those in the *Advanced Equipment* chapter later.

Chapter Ten

PRIMING

SAFETY FIRST!

Always wear protective glasses when reloading. Primers are designed to explode when impacted, and by definition, you're using force to press them into place. Also, make sure that the open mouth of the cartridge case is facing away from you when inserting primers!

We'll cover priming cartridge cases from a "getting started" point of view. If you own something like a Dillon Precision Super 1050 progressive reloading press, you've spent somewhere approaching $2,000 and are auto-priming like there's no tomorrow. Rock on! If you have no idea what I'm talking about, no worries, we'll talk about progressive reloading presses in the *Advanced Equipment* chapter later.

Let's take a look at a few different ways to insert new primers into your cartridge cases. We'll show you how they work and discuss some of the pros and cons so you can decide which method is right for you.

We'll skip the budget method of hammering primers into place with a mallet, as that generally results in lost fingers and your quick enrollment onto the terrorist watch list.

SAFETY FIRST!

Avoid handling primers with your bare hands. The oils from your hands can interfere with proper ignition later and you really don't want to be touching nasty explosive stuff. You may have to flip one over by hand now and then, and that's OK. Just avoid excessive handling.

Since primers are technically explosives, and potentially dangerous, this is the perfect place to stop and explain a situation you will most certainly encounter as you start to reload.

CRIMPED PRIMERS

Crimping primers is a process manufacturers use to ensure that the primer will not move or back out of the primer pocket. The insanely practical definition is that the metal around the outside of the primer pocket is "jammed" (like that technical term?) in such a way that it puts pressure around the edge of the primer. It's a little bit like putting a picture in a pre-fab picture frame. You can just set the picture in the frame and it will probably stay there under normal use. Or, you can mash those little tabs towards the center so they "jam" the picture into the frame opening and hold it firmly in place.

Most of the time, you'll only encounter crimped primers with military brass like 5.56mm. 7.62 or maybe 9mm. But crimps appear in other brands of ammo also. Never fear, the vast majority of ammo you buy won't have crimps.

Why should you care about this? Because the crimps that press in towards the center of the primer pocket make the pocket just a tad smaller. This means that you can't just push a new primer into place as the exterior of the hole is too small. You need to remove the crimp first.

When you start to prime a batch of brass cases, ideally you will remove cases with crimped primer pockets first. The problem is that crimps are hard to spot with the naked eye. Over time, you'll start to recognize which brands of cartridge cases are likely to have crimps and you can spot them by looking at the manufacturer stamps on the bottom of the case.

No matter how carefully you inspect your brass cases prior to priming, it's only a matter of time before a crimped case makes its way into your batch of brass that's ready to prime. As long as you're attentive to the priming task, this isn't a big deal. With any of the priming methods we're going to discuss, you'll be able to feel a "hard stop" when trying to insert a primer into a crimped primer pocket. If the insertion feels abnormally difficult, STOP! Don't try to force the primer into place. Remember, it's designed to explode when crushed. You really, really don't want that to happen. And you especially don't want one exploding primer to ignite others loaded in the tool you're using. This is one of the reasons to always wear eye protection when reloading.

> ## SAFETY FIRST!
>
> *If you feel resistance when inserting primers, STOP! Refer to the manufacturer instructions for your specific priming tool to see how to safely identify the problem. You might have just encountered a crimped primer pocket that needs to be un-crimped before re-priming.*

The good news is that you can still reload cartridge cases with crimped primers. You just need to remove the crimp first. We'll talk about a couple of tools that will help you do that in the *Advanced Equipment* chapter.

For now, I want you to be aware of what crimped primers are and how to spot them. Most importantly, remember not to try to force anything into place when reloading. Ever! If something doesn't feel right, stop and evaluate.

HAND PRIMING

Hand priming tools allow you to complete the priming step as a separate operation. You don't need a reloading press or bench.

There's another benefit of hand priming tools. You can control the pressure and depth of priming fairly well as you are pressing the new primer into place with a hand tool, not a hydraulic machine. After a couple hundred, you'll develop a feel that tells you primers are seated correctly. Hand priming tools are also great for catching cartridge cases with crimped primer pockets. You'll easily feel the abnormal resistance when you encounter a crimped primer pocket.

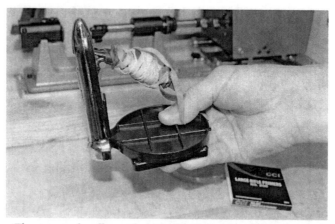

The easy and spill proof way to load your hand priming tool is to hold it upside down over the package of primers, then turn the whole mess upside down. Now companies are making square priming tool trays so this is easier to do without spilling. I've done a little "quality" modification to this hand tool by wrapping about a hundred rubber bands around the handle to make it a bit more comfortable to use.

Here's how they work.

Most hand primers have a tray that's large enough to hold a box of 100 primers. Holding your opened box of primers, turn the

Just a gentle shake-shake and the ridges in this tray will flip all the primers over so they are oriented open side up and ready to load. There are a few still not flipped in this photo, so a little more shaking is required.

hand priming tool tray upside down over the primer packaging tray, then flip the whole assembly.

If done correctly, you've now got all 100 primers in the hand primer tool tray. You'll notice the tray is ridged or textured. That allows you to gently shake the tray until all the primers are facing upwards, so they will insert correctly.

When all the primers are oriented correctly, put the cover over the tray to prevent primers from spilling and flipping.

Many hand priming tools, like the Lee Auto Prime shown here, use removable shell holders to hold the case still while a primer is pressed into place. These shell holders are sized to caliber, so you simply insert the correct one for the batch you're going to prime. Once you've got the right shell holder in place, primers loaded and cover in place, you're ready to prime.

Slide a cartridge case into the holder, squeeze the hand tool and drive the primer into place. You'll quickly learn the ideal angle at which to operate your hand primer so that the next-in-line primer falls into place from gravity.

INSANELY PRACTICAL TIP!

*Don't throw that empty primer box away!
Keep it in view, while you are actually re-prim-
ing. It's a great safety check that reminds you
of exactly what primers you are using in a
particular batch. Primers can "look" identical,
but are not. Different brands have different
performance. Magnum primers which explode
with more enthusiasm look the same as regular
ones. Rifle primers look just like pistol primers.
Keep your package in view until you're completely finished with the task.*

*I'm doing this at about a 45 degree angle for two
reasons. First, gravity will feed the primers. Second, the
open end of the cartridge case is pointed away from my
face!*

Remove the case from the shell holder and repeat.

Once you get the hang of the process, you'll be able to handle
hundreds of primings per hour.

SAFETY FIRST!

Angle the hand priming tool so that the open mouth of the case faces away from you. In the event a primer does ignite, at least the "blast" will not be headed towards your face.

BENCH PRIMING

Think of a bench primer as a tool that offers more leverage and consistency than a hand priming tool, but less force than a reloading press priming accessory. The bench priming tool still gives you some mechanical advantage over the primer insertion process, but has enough "feel" that you can easily catch cases with crimped primer pockets.

The process for using a bench mounted priming tool is pretty much the same as for a hand priming tool. Instead of squeezing a primer into place, you use a lever to press the primer into place. It's definitely easier on the hands!

This RCBS bench priming tool comes with large and small primer tubes to automate the process. The longer lever gives more leverage than a hand priming tool.

About Primer Tubes

A number of priming tools like bench primers, single stage reloading press priming accessories and progressive reloading presses use primer tubes to hold multiple primers and feed them singly into the priming device.

These are a neat invention. They have a removable pin at one end to close it off and a flexible plastic "nozzle" at the other that is just smaller than a primer. Not only do they hold a stack of

Here's an RCBS primer tray. Hold the base of the tray over the open package of primers and turn both over. Now you end up with primers in the tray as shown here. A gentle shake or swirl and they'll flip over so they are base down and open side up.

primers, they help you pick them up. Just push the plastic "nozzle" over a primer and it will be pushed into the tube. The plastic tip will prevent it from falling back out. The clip on the other end of the tube will keep that end sealed. Tubes come in two sizes for large and small primers.

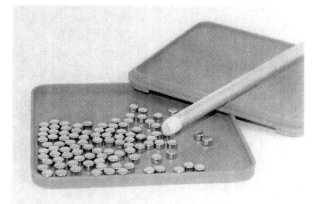

A primer pick up tube has a flexible plastic end that is a hair smaller than the primer.

You will need a primer tray to help you flip the primers so they are oriented in the same direction. Just like with the trays in hand priming tools, you empty a box of primers onto the tray. Gentle movement of the tray will cause them to orient with the open end up. Now put the lid on the tray, flip it upside down and remove the base. You'll have all the primers facing you bottom side up, ready to capture with the primer tube.

SINGLE STAGE RELOADING PRESS PRIMING

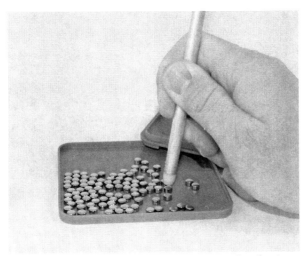

To load the tube with primers, just press the plastic nozzle over them one at a time. The plastic prevents them from falling back out.

Many single stage reloading presses offer attachments that allow you to insert a primer using the hydraulic pressure of the press itself. I have to say, I'm not a big fan. It works fine, but for me, it's a cumbersome process.

Some allow one-at-a-time primer seating while others allow attachment of a primer tube that facilitates semi-automated feeding of primers into the press.

As with a bench priming tool, you need to use a primer tray to orient the primers bottom up. Then you pick up a batch of primers with a primer tube. With each stroke of the press, you can activate the priming mechanism to seat the primer in the case. In the case of this Lyman press and priming accessory, you push the priming arm into a hollow cutout in the press piston and lower the cartridge case onto the primer.

The advantages are that you are using the power and leverage of the reloading press. You can also use the same shell holder

This Lyman single stage press has a priming tool attachment that allows you to use the leverage of the press to seat a primer. You can also mount a primer tube to automatically "place" primers into the seater.

that you use for other reloading operations, so you don't need to purchase a whole set of separate shell holders. Perhaps most importantly, the priming operation is completed farther away from your hands and face in the event something goes wrong.

The disadvantage is (in my opinion) that it's a more cumbersome operation. There's no harm in trying this method out, especially if your single stage press came equipped with the capability.

PROGRESSIVE RELOADING PRESS PRIMING

I won't spend a lot of time explaining "how" to prime using a progressive reloading machine. If you have one of those, you already know. Instead, I'll consider the benefits of priming this way so you can make a more informed decision as to whether to shell out some big bucks for progressive reloading equipment.

As with the single stage press option we just discussed, you'll need a way to get the primers into the reloading press. Lee Precision progressive machines feed from a tray like hand priming tools, so that's simple. Other types of reloading presses use tubes to hold primers. These work exactly the same as tubes for bench primers and single stage press priming tubes. You can even buy power tools that automatically fill primer tubes for you. Extravagant? Not if you're reloading thousands of cartridges at a time!

On this Hornady progressive reloading press, a primer tube (back) feeds primers one at a time. As the next case rotates into place, a piston pushes the primer into place. It's luxurious!

Once the primers are in the tube, and attached to your progressive press, you're off to the races. With each down stroke (or up stroke depending on the make of your press) you're inserting a new primer. The best part is that with a progressive press, you're also resizing, decapping, belling the case mouth, powder charging, bullet seating and crimping. So with a progressive reloading press, priming is no longer a separate operation. Each pull of the handle completes a reloaded cartridge. Nifty.

We'll talk about progressive reloading presses more in the *Advanced Equipment* chapter.

Which Method Should You Use?

In my opinion, you can't go wrong investing in a hand priming tool. For somewhere between $20 and $75 you'll have a tool for life. I've got single stage and progressive presses, but still use my hand priming tools all the time. Whether it be smaller reloading batches or the convenience of getting a pile of cases ready to reload at my leisure, I've gotten my money's worth out of my hand priming tools.

Chapter Eleven

CASE MOUTH BELLING

If you're reloading a bottleneck cartridge, I've got good news for you. You're done with this step! That's because resizing dies for bottleneck cartridges include a "ball" on the decapping spindle that opens the case mouth to the proper dimension. So when you resize the cartridge, you're also opening the case mouth. Piece of cake, right?

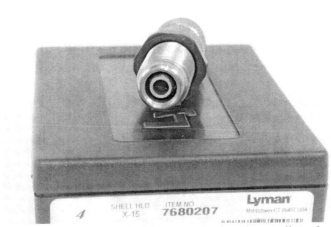

Here's the business end of the expander die. The spindle in the middle is hollow so powder can flow through it if you want to combine steps.

If you're reloading straight wall cartridges, then you do need to complete this step. Fortunately, it's a really simple one. No lubrication, hardware store trips or hocus-pocus spells.

Reloading die sets for straight wall cartridges generally come with a case mouth expander die. Expander dies have an insert that opens the mouth of a cartridge case just a tiny bit so that you can easily seat a bullet. It works like any other die.

- ▷ Make sure you have a shell holder for the right caliber.

- ▷ Screw the expander die in place.

- ▷ Slide a cartridge case into the shell holder.

- ▷ Carefully raise the piston and case to the expander die.

- ▷ Adjust the die and/or insert depth until the very edge of the mouth is barely opened.

- ▷ Lock the die and insert in place.

It's important to expand the case mouth to the absolute minimum — here's why. What actually holds a bullet in place until it's fired is *case neck tension*. Technically, it's not the crimping

Can you see how this case is expanded at the mouth? Nope? Exactly! You want to just barely open it — only enough so that a bullet can be inserted cleanly. This one is lopsided as it's not been pressed into place yet.

step we'll get to later. You want the bullet to encounter plenty of friction as it is seated in the cartridge case. The friction between the sides of the projectile and interior walls of the case are what hold it in place.

If you open the case too much, you reduce the surface area for case neck tension and your bullets may not stay firmly seated.

SAFETY FIRST!

Bullet setback is an issue to be aware of. If there is not enough case neck tension, bullets can be pushed back into the case, deeper than they should be. This results in less volume in the case when the powder charge ignites which can cause dangerously high pressures. It's always a good idea to press on a bullet to make sure it's firmly seated and gripped by the case. Some calibers, like .357 Sig, are more prone to this issue because they have a short neck and less surface area for proper case neck tension. Bullet setback can also occur as a result of repeated chambering of the same round. Each time it's slammed into the chamber, more force is applied to the bullet, which can eventually drive it into the case. I mention this for general awareness purposes. Develop a habit of keeping any eye out for bullet setback. If a bullet looks like it is pressed abnormally far into the case, don't shoot it! Use your bullet puller to take it apart and start over.

If you don't open the case mouth quite enough, you might cause the cartridge case to crush when you force a bullet into it. Or you might damage the bullet itself as the base and sides get scraped. If you reload lead bullets, you may cause lead and bullet lubricant to shave off and get all over the outside of your case.

So when you are adjusting the expander die, have the same type of bullet handy that you are about to reload. Test one case and see if the base of the bullet just barely fits into the case mouth.

There's one more thing worth mentioning here. Depending on what starting equipment you buy, you might have the option of combining the powder drop and mouth expansion steps. Some

This is the top end of the expander die. I show this to illustrate how some are hollow and give you the option to load powder during the same operation.

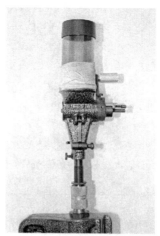

Here's the same expander die installed in the press with a powder dispenser mounted to the top of the die. When the case is pushed up into the die, just pull the powder dispenser handle and the right powder charge is dropped through the die and into the case.

dies have a hollow insert. This insert still expands the case mouth, but being hollow, it's designed to mount a powder dispenser on top. So you can raise the case into the die, which expands the mouth. While the case is still in the die, drop the powder charge into the case. It's just a way to save a step!

Chapter Twelve

POWDER CHARGING

"Charging" is such an aggressive word isn't it? All it really means is "filling." It's not as intimidating as it sounds. For purposes of reloading, charging simply refers to putting new powder back in your empty cartridge case.

SAFETY FIRST!

Many powders on the market have "similar" names and/or numbers but they are not interchangeable. Never, ever, ever make substitutions for "similar" alternatives!

There are more powders on the market than lobbyists in Washington, DC. It's critical to use the right one, and exactly the right amount, as they are all designed with different burning rates dependent on the cartridge and projectile type. Burning rate is exactly what it says — an indication of how fast the powder itself is consumed in the burning process. Powder manufacturers use all sorts of tricks to carefully control burning rates. The shape of powder kernels and chemicals can impact the burn rate of powders.

Sometimes beginners equate burn rate of a powder and expected velocity of the bullet when fired, and that's not exactly how it works. To understand a little more about powders, you have to understand the concept of a pressure curve. This book is a starter guide, so we'll provide a simplified description.

ABOUT PRESSURE

When powder ignites in an enclosed space like a cartridge, the chemical reaction creates a volume of gas. Pressure comes into play as the expanding volume of gas has nowhere to go, so pressure increases. At some point, the pressure of the gas exceeds the force of friction holding the bullet in place and the barrel and the bullet is driven out.

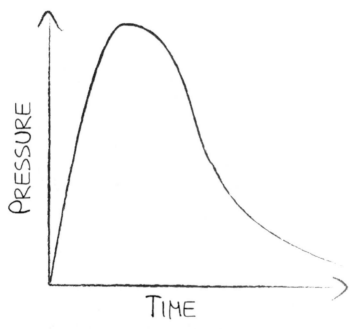

Pressure curves look something like this. But the shape, timing and spike vary with powder type, amount, caliber, primer type and lots of other factors.

However, there can be too much of a good thing. While increased pressure can create increased bullet velocity, there are a million "it depends" exceptions. And this is exactly where the concept of pressure curve comes into play.

When the firing pin smashes and ignites the primer, it lights the powder in the cartridge, and a very rapid burn and gas expansion occurs. Pressure builds very, very quickly. As the bullet starts to move, pressure falls. This is because the space available to the expanding gas becomes larger as the bullet travels down the barrel. Think of the available space as a cylinder that becomes longer. Ultimately, after the bullet leaves the barrel, pressure falls to zero, as nothing is left to contain the gas.

You'll find that small pistol cartridges, like .32 ACP for example, use faster burning powders. Pressure needs to develop quickly to get maximum benefit before the bullet leaves the barrel. At the other end of the spectrum, larger rifle calibers tend to use slower burning powders. They are designed to keep burning and creating expanding gas, while the bullet travels down the longer barrel. Since the burn rate is slower, pressure doesn't spike as high at the peak, but it develops over a longer period of time.

SAFETY FIRST!

Using the wrong amount or type of propellant can blow up your gun and/or injure people, so be careful. Always use the exact powder called for in the load recipe and stay within the upper and lower charge weight limits specified.

The trick with getting safe, good performance out of any caliber reload is making sure the pressure curve is right for the job. The burn rate of the powder (and rate at which it creates expanding gas) has to be in harmony with the volume of the cartridge, barrel length, projectile weight and designed strength of the gun. Fortunately, you don't have to worry about this if you stick to published load recipes in reloading manuals. I cover pressure curve concepts here to illustrate the importance of making sure all variables like powder type, primer type, bullet weight and cartridge type are carefully followed.

SAFETY FIRST!

Too much powder!

If you overcharge a cartridge case, or put too much powder in it, you risk increasing that pressure spike we talked about to dangerous levels. While it may be tempting to try to "make your bullets go faster" don't do it! If you exceed the maximum quantity of powder specified in a reputable reloading manual, you risk blowing up your gun, injury and even death.

Too little powder!

Not using enough powder is just as dangerous. If you load less than the minimum specified in a reputable reloading manual, you risk not developing enough pressure to push the bullet out of the cartridge or barrel. If you follow that (called a squib load) with another shot, you have just fired another bullet into a blocked barrel, potentially causing an explosion. If something doesn't sound quite right after firing a shot, don't shoot again! Stop and follow your gun manufacturers procedures for unloading and checking your gun.

HOW TO MEASURE POWDER CHARGES

Reloading recipes almost always use weight as a unit of measure to specify the amount of powder to include in a specific cartridge. Since cartridges are sensitive to very small fluctuations in powder weight, a different measurement unit is used — grains. A grain sounds like it might refer to a "piece" of powder, but it's just a weight measurement — 1/7000th of a pound to be exact.

Since it's so important to get the weight exactly right, I recommend checking the accuracy of your scale every time you start a reloading session. If you have an old-fashioned beam scale, check and make sure it balances with all the settings at zero. If you have a digital scale, use the included calibration weight to make sure it's reading accurately. Be sure to keep an eye on your batteries too. When batteries get low, digital scales can do wonky things.

Store your powder on a different shelf from where you work. When actively reloading, have only the one powder container in use on your reloading bench. That way, you'll be absolutely sure of which powder is in your powder dispenser.

So let's talk about a couple of different ways to charge your cases.

In the basic equipment section, I mentioned the powder scoops that are available in different sizes. While seemingly handy, I prefer to avoid them because (to me) they don't provide much benefit for very little cost savings. You would need a drawer full of different size scoops to cover every volume/weight combination. Even if you have the right scoop, the measurement is still going to be less precise than what you'll get with a powder dispenser and scale. A powder dispenser is also faster, which is a big deal if you're reloading more than a box or two of cartridges. So here, we're going to focus on using a hand-operated powder dispenser.

Most powder dispensers operate on the same general principle.

I've been using the Lyman No. 55 Powder Dispenser shown in the photos here for a long, long time. That's why the bottom is all wrapped up with athletic tape. I wore the threads on the powder reservoir down to nothing, so it wouldn't screw into the base anymore. Athletic tape, duct tape, it all works the same.

This Lyman model, like others, can mount different ways according to your desired method of use. It's got a clamp on the back, so you can just mount it to a

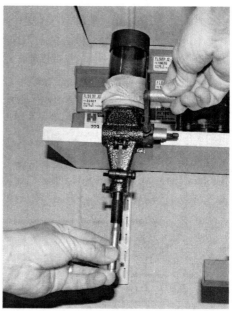

Powder dispenser in action. Just hold the case up to the beveled tube and pull the lever. Couldn't be easier.

shelf. Or, as we discussed in the *Case Mouth Belling* chapter, you can screw the chute of the powder dispenser right into the top of a mouth expanding die. I would recommend using the shelf method when you start to keep each step separate. After you've expanded the mouths of a bunch of cases, then worry about the powder charging step.

The principle is simple. You fill a reservoir (that's a fancy name for the big plastic hopper) with your powder of choice. The reservoir feeds into a handle-operated dispenser. Within the dispenser body is a cleverly designed cylindrical cavity. This cavity features a movable "plug" that's called a metering bar. It's made of three interconnected bars — a large segment, medium and small. They are independently controlled by finger screws and together determine how much of the cavity is taken up by the plug. The open space remaining determines how much powder is allowed to drop into the cavity from the reservoir each time the handle is operated. By sliding the three metering bars — large to get close, medium to get closer and small to get fine volume measurement, you can size the cavity to drop the exact powder charge you want — down to the tenth of a grain.

Adjusting the cavity with the metering bars is a trial and error method. While you'll be able to eyeball your way close after a couple

Note the three meter bars to precisely adjust the powder quantity. The large metering bar is the biggest cylinder while the medium and small rest on top of that.

of reloading sessions, the first time will take a few tries. If you're reloading a pistol cartridge, you can probably start with the large bar close. Open the medium bar a bit, drop a charge into a shell casing and pour the powder into your scale pan. When you see the actual weight, you'll know whether to adjust your metering bars more open or close. Repeat the process until it's set to drop the exact weight you want. Most powder dispensers have a

The knocker on the powder dispenser. Sounds technical doesn't it?

finger screw to "lock" the metering bars in place once you get them set right, so be sure to fasten that down too.

Powder dispensers have a way of "settling" into a groove, so be sure to drop a number of charges, weighing each one, before you start filling up lots of cases. You may find you have to readjust your measuring bars as the powder settles. I find it also helps to keep your powder reservoir fairly full. If you start full and let it get to almost empty, you may find that your charges are inconsistent as the powder level goes down. It's a gravity thing — there's not much powder left to push down into the metering chamber.

Oh, that little hinged thing hanging on the front? It's called... a knocker. Yep, really. You flip it up until it smacks into the body of the powder dispenser and it shakes loose any powder that might have stuck to the inside of the measure. It helps ensure that you get a consistent does dropped every time.

The powder loading step is where reloading trays really come in handy. It stinks to spill powder all over your work area when you inadvertently knock over filled cases. By the way, if you do, throw away the spilled powder and start over. Don't try to put it back in the case or reuse it. You don't know the exact quantity once it spilled and you don't know what other contaminants got mixed in.

After I bell a bunch of cases, I toss them in a plastic container. I pull one out at a time and dispense the powder into it.

Invest about $15 or so on one of those flexible lamps like you used to use in high school or college. Mount it on your workbench so you have plenty of light shining on your loading area. This makes it much easier to see inside the recently charged cartridge cases to visually verify the powder charge.

After the powder drops in, I take a look in the case to make sure it looks about right and then place the "charged" case into a reloading tray. Every five or ten cases, I'll dump the powder contents into the scale to make sure that my dispenser is still dropping the right amount of powder. You can use a simple powder funnel

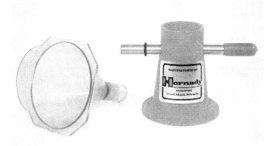

*A couple of really handy accessories: a powder funnel
(left) and powder trickler (right). The powder tricker
"drips" tiny amounts of powder into your scale pan to get
the perfect charge weight.*

to pour from the scale pan back into the case.

When the tray is full, usually with 50 charged cartridge cases, I hold it up to a light and scan down the rows of cartridge cases to visually verify that all the charges look the same. Consider this another safety check to make sure none of the cases have no charge or an overcharge.

This method is perfectly acceptable for volume reloading of rifle and pistol cartridges. A good powder dispenser will get you consistently within 1/10th of a grain of the desired powder charge weight.

For any given caliber, there are lots of powder and powder weight choices. I like to pick a powder type and weight (within published limits) that fills the cartridge case most of the way. It's easy to visually verify that the correct amount of powder has been dispensed. With the right combination, it's also nearly impossible to overcharge a cartridge, as the powder would literally overflow the case.

If you want to be super precise for accuracy competition loads, you can certainly weigh each powder charge individually. While not practical for volume pistol reloads, it can work well for smaller batches of rifle cartridges.

Powder trickling. In this photo, I dumped less than I wanted with a powder dispenser and am using a powder trickler to get exactly to 38.0 grains for a .308 Winchester load.

What I do for these scenarios is set my powder dispenser to deliver a little less than the desired charge weight. Dispense and pour that into the scale pan. Now, you can use a powder trickler to dribble small amounts of the same powder into the scale pan while it's still on the scale. When the weight is perfect, pour the contents of the scale pan into each cartridge case using a funnel.

SAFETY FIRST!

Working with powder is serious business. Never, ever, ever mix or combine powders. Better yet, don't experiment on your own. Always follow published loading data and never exceed published minimum or maximum charge amounts. If you make a mistake, or think you might have made a mistake. Stop! Undo what you did and start over. A bullet puller is an indispensable tool as it's far better to take apart a round you're unsure of them risk consequences on the range.

Chapter Thirteen

BULLET SEATING

Seating the bullet simply means pressing it into the cartridge case to the proper depth. Precise seating depth is important for a number of reasons.

▷ The cartridge has to fit properly in the chamber and/or magazine, so it can't be too long.

▷ The bullet is designed to be a certain distance from the start of the rifling in the barrel. If it presses too far into the grooves of the rifling, dangerously high pressure conditions can result.

▷ Pressing the bullet too far into the case can also create dangerously high pressures.

▷ If a revolver cartridge is too long, the bullet might extend out of the cylinder and prevent it from turning.

You'll notice that every load recipe in a reputable reloading manual also specifies a bullet weight, bullet type (shape) and cartridge overall length.

It's important to use the exact weight of bullet specified for a given load because the powder charge as been developed to push that weight of projectile to the desired velocity with the proper pressure.

The bullet type matters because for any given weight, a bullet might have a different length. If a bullet has a long and pointy nose, it might weigh exactly the same as one with a stubby flat point. But since they are different lengths, when you push it into a cartridge from the top, the seating depth can be very different.

The Cartridge Overall Length (C.O.A.L. or C.O.L.) is specified for each type and weight bullet combination as a way to control the interior volume of the cartridge case. Any given published load recipe is carefully developed making an assumption about the volume in the cartridge case. If a bullet is pushed farther into the case, there is less interior volume. If the same amount of powder ignites in a smaller volume, pressure will be have to be higher. Likewise, if a bullet is not pressed in deep enough, there will be more available volume in the case, and pressure will be lower.

SEATING DEPTH ISSUES

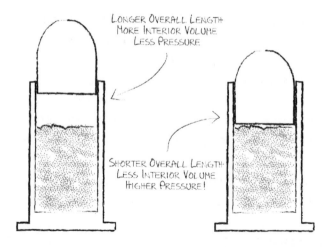

LONGER OVERALL LENGTH
MORE INTERIOR VOLUME
LESS PRESSURE

SHORTER OVERALL LENGTH
LESS INTERIOR VOLUME
HIGHER PRESSURE!

For example, a recipe for a .45 ACP load might specify an overall cartridge length of 1.212 inches for a 185 grain jacketed hollow point bullet, but a length of 1.155 inches for a 185 grain flat point jacketed match bullet. This is because the two bullets are different lengths although they weigh the same.

SAFETY FIRST!

Remember, we're talking about peak pressure levels in the tens of thousands of pounds per square inch, so it's really, really important to pay close attention to the details for each specific load. Always check the bullet weight, bullet type and cartridge overall length to make sure they are within published guidelines.

HOW TO SEAT A BULLET

Most seating dies actually perform two functions: seating and crimping. If you adjust your die and press exactly, and your brass cartridge cases are all the same length, then you can do both steps at once with good reliability.

But just because you can, doesn't mean that you should. Here's why. Seating the bullet involves pressing it into the cartridge case.

Seating dies have a removable plug that adjusts up and down in the die body to set the exact seating depth.

We know from previous discussion that this should be a tight fit, with the exception of the case mouth which has been opened just a bit to allow the bullet to get started. When you're crimping at the same time, you're applying inward pressure while you are applying downward pressure to seat the bullet. It's like putting a cork in a wine bottle where the bottle neck continuously gets smaller while you're trying to push the cork in.

If you are reloading softer lead or plated bullets, it's possible to create a small bulge in the cartridge if the die adjustments are not perfect. The force of the seating plug against the pressure from the crimp can squash the bullet to the point of expanding the case itself. This bulge can interfere with reliable chambering of your cartridges. I'm not confirming or denying, but I might have learned about this the hard way.

I prefer to handle seating and crimping as separate steps. Doing these operations separately is a lot more forgiving and adjustment of the die for each step is much easier.

Depending on the caliber, seating dies may come with more than one insert. You'll notice that one insert comes with a flat recessed end for flat point and wadcutter bullet designs. The other will be shaped for a rounded bullet.

Here's how I do the seating step:

> First, make sure your seating die insert is right for the bullet type you are loading — rounded nose or flat point.

> Loosen the seating insert in your die way, way out. We don't want it screwed in far enough to reach a bullet yet.

> Insert the shell holder in the piston of your press.

An inside view of a competition quality seating die. The spindle adjusts up and down via micrometer settings to specify the exact depth at which to seat the bullet. Image: RCBS.

▷ Put an empty case in the shell holder and raise the piston of your press all the way up.

▷ Now, screw the die into the press until you feel the die just touch the cartridge case that is raised into the die area. Loosen the whole die about a full turn to make sure that the die body does not touch the cartridge case. The die body is shaped on the inside to provide the crimp, so if it's screwed in too far, it will be crimping your case. When you're sure the die is not touching your cartridge case, use the die locking ring to fasten the die body in place.

▷ Lower the piston and remove the empty brass.

▷ Take a cartridge case, with its powder charge, and place it in the shell holder.

▷ Place a bullet in the mouth of the case.

▷ Raise the press all the way.

▷ Now tighten the seating die insert until you feel it touch the bullet.

▷ Lower the press piston.

▷ Tighten the seating die insert a couple of turns and raise the press again. This should start to press your bullet into the case. Lower the piston and check the length of your cartridge with your calipers. Keep adjusting the seating stem and measuring the cartridge until you have got it set for the overall length you want. Many dies have a locking ring for the seating stem also to make sure it stays at the desired setting.

▷ Proceed with seating the remainder of the bullets in your batch. Check the length of one every now and then to make sure your settings are correct.

Chapter Fourteen

BULLET CRIMPING

Crimping can be a bit of a misnomer. It sounds like it's the process of squeezing the bullet into place in the cartridge case, but it's really not.

If previous steps are done correctly, there is no need to squash the brass against the seated bullet to "squeeze" the bullet firmly into place. Remember, in the *Case Mouth Belling* chapter, we talked about how case neck tension holds the bullet firmly in the brass cartridge. When a bullet is seated in a properly re-sized case, there's already a lot of tension holding the bullet still.

TAPER CRIMP

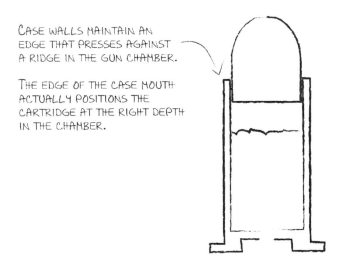

CASE WALLS MAINTAIN AN EDGE THAT PRESSES AGAINST A RIDGE IN THE GUN CHAMBER.

THE EDGE OF THE CASE MOUTH ACTUALLY POSITIONS THE CARTRIDGE AT THE RIGHT DEPTH IN THE CHAMBER.

For most semi-automatic pistol cartridges, crimping simply refers to the process of removing the "flare" of the cartridge case mouth, which we created in the *Case Mouth Belling* step. This is known as taper crimping.

ROLL CRIMP

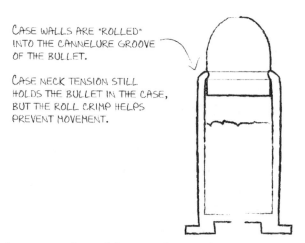

CASE WALLS ARE "ROLLED" INTO THE CANNELURE GROOVE OF THE BULLET.

CASE NECK TENSION STILL HOLDS THE BULLET IN THE CASE, BUT THE ROLL CRIMP HELPS PREVENT MOVEMENT.

For other cartridges, like revolver calibers such as .38 Special, .357 Magnum, .44 Special and .44 Magnum to name a few, crimping can do more than just remove the "flare." Known as "roll crimping," this process can be used to push the edge of the brass case mouth into the bullet itself, helping lock it into place.

I know this may sound a bit confusing, but we'll make sense of it - I promise! To really understand the crimping step, and differences between taper and roll crimps, we need to take a slight diversion and talk about headspace.

This taper crimp die is hollow. It's shaped to press the brass cartridge case mouth back into shape after the belling and seating steps.

HEAD SPACE

Headspace is a big and complex topic that we don't need to fully digest here. For purposes of learning reloading concepts, let's use a simple definition.

Think of headspace as the amount of "free space" between the breech face and the bottom of the cartridge case when it's loaded in the chamber of a gun. A bullet has to be a little bit smaller than the chamber of the gun so it can be inserted and then extracted after firing, so there is a little bit of wiggle room. The headspace is more or less the amount of front to back wiggle room.

Technically speaking, headspace is not a measurement of the "free space" but rather a distance from the breech face to differ-

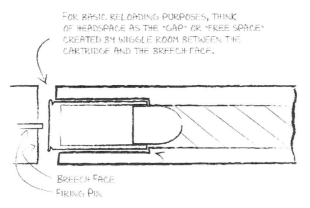

WHAT IS HEADSPACE?

FOR BASIC RELOADING PURPOSES, THINK OF HEADSPACE AS THE "GAP" OR "FREE SPACE" CREATED BY WIGGLE ROOM BETWEEN THE CARTRIDGE AND THE BREECH FACE.

BREECH FACE
FIRING PIN

ent points depending on the type of cartridge in question. Some calibers measure headspace from the breech face to the cartridge rim, others to the cartridge mouth, and so on. From a reloaders perspective, just understand that we want to manage the amount of free play between the breech face and cartridge.

GUN WORDS Explained!

Just to be clear on terminology, the breech face is the flat part of the bolt, slide or frame of a gun where the firing pin hole is located. With semi-automatic guns, the breech face is part of the slide. As the slide moves forward, the breech face presses up against the bottom of the cartridge. The same concept applies with bolt action rifles. With a revolver, the breech face is actually part of the frame behind the cylinder.

The chamber of the gun (with the breech closed) and the dimensions of the cartridge determine the headspace. If a cartridge is way too short, there will be a lot of front to back play, and therefore more headspace. If it's too long, the bolt or cylinder won't close properly because the base of the cartridge is sticking out too far.

In addition to the size of the cartridge, there is another factor that determines headspace. Cartridges are always "positioned" in a chamber by one element of their shape.

STRAIGHT WALL CARTRIDGE HEADSPACE

THE END OF THE CARTRIDGE CASE MOUTH
PRESSES UP AGAINST A RIDGE LIKE THIS
IN THE CHAMBER OF THE GUN TO SET THE
"DEPTH" OF THE CARTRIDGE.

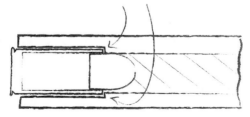

Straight wall pistol cartridges are positioned by the cartridge case mouth pressing up against a ridge in the chamber.

RIMMED CARTRIDGE HEADSPACE

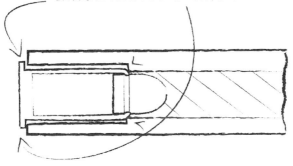

THE CARTRIDGE IS HELD AT THE RIGHT
POSITION BY THE RIM ON THE CARTRIDGE
ITSELF, WHICH BUTTS UP AGAINST THE
BARREL AT THE REAR OF THE CHAMBER.

Rimmed cartridges are positioned by the rim of the cartridge case preventing the case from moving further into the chamber.

BOTTLENECK CARTRIDGE HEADSPACE

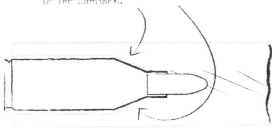

WITH A BOTTLENECK CARTRIDGE LIKE THE
.223 REMINGTON, THE CARTRIDGE CASE IS
FIXED IN POSITION BY THE SHOULDER OF
THE CASE MEETING A RIDGE ON THE INSIDE
OF THE CHAMBER.

Rimless bottleneck cartridges are positioned by the shoulder of the case pressing into the chamber itself.

There are some minor variances, but for the most part, these are the primary methods that help determine headspace.

Bear with me, because here's where the type of crimp comes into play.

A straight wall pistol cartridge requires a taper crimp because there must be a hard edge to the cartridge case mouth — that's the part that butts up against the ridge in the chamber to position the cartridge in the right place. For example, if you apply a roll crimp to a 9mm cartridge, there is no "hard stop" and the cartridge will be able to move back and forth in the chamber. If it moves too far forward, the firing pin may not reach the primer with enough force to fire the cartridge. Or, if there is too much space between the base of the cartridge and the breech face, the cartridge will stretch lengthwise when fired, thereby creating a dangerous situation where the case may rupture and vent hot gas back towards the shooter.

Left to right: A lead bullet with a crimping groove, a .300 Blackout bullet with crimping groove, a .308 bullet with a cannelure and a .308 bullet with no cannelure.

On the other hand, with a caliber where the headspace is determined by a rim, like the .38 Special, or by the position of the shoulder, as with the .223 Remington, a taper crimp is not required. In these cases, you can choose to roll crimp the bullet in place. If you are reloading bottleneck case rifle bullets, make sure to read the rifle cartridge crimping section coming up — there are some important things to know!

A cannelure groove circles the bullet at the exact position where the case mouth ends. This allows the case mouth to be "roll crimped" so it presses into the groove. This creates a locking effect that helps prevent the bullet moving in or out. As an example, revolvers with heavy recoil benefit from this as the cartridges in the cylinder experience an aggressive recoil force when a cartridge is fired. Without a good, solid crimp, bullets can move deeper into their cases, or start to pull out of their cases.

TAPER CRIMPING

In the previous chapter, I mentioned that I usually perform seating and crimping as separate steps. Since the bullets are already seated, I'll remove the seating stem from my seating and crimping die so there is one less variable to worry about.

A taper crimp is easy. The biggest problem that new taper-crimpers face is applying too much crimp. All that's really necessary is to apply just enough crimp to remove the belling from the cartridge case after a bullet is seated. Think of a proper taper crimp as just making the walls of the case straight and parallel again.

Too much taper crimp can definitely be a bad thing. It can lead to reliability issues for cartridges like 9mm, .40 S&W and .45 ACP that headspace on the case mouth. It can cause bullets to do weird things like tumble and fly sideways. Simply put, no good can come from over-crimping your cartridges and more is definitely not better in this step.

The basic process is simple.

▷ Make sure you have the right shell holder in your reloading press.

▷ Insert a cartridge with a seated bullet in place.

▷ Raise the piston of your press all the way up.

▷ Now, screw the seating die body into the press until you feel it contact the mouth of the case.

▷ Check your particular die instructions as those will give you some guidance on how much to tighten the die once you feel it hit the cartridge case mouth. Usually you will only tighten it an additional ¼ of a turn to achieve the desired crimp.

▷ Remove and visually inspect your crimped cartridge to make sure it's what you wanted. You can also use your calipers to double check the diameter of the case mouth area to make sure it's correct for the caliber you are reloading. Your reloading manual will provide that dimension.

ROLL CRIMPING

The steps to roll crimp are exactly the same as those for taper crimping, but the result is different. Instead of just trying to remove the flare in the cartridge case mouth, we actually want to drive the edges of the case mouth into the cannelure grooves of the bullet.

You'll see, and use, roll crimping a lot on rimmed cartridges like .357 Magnum or .44 Magnum. One reason is that when a revolver recoils, it will have an effect on the cartridges remaining in the cylinder. We want the bullets in those cartridges to stay put and not move further into the case, or start to creep out of the case. The roll crimp helps prevent that.

Within reason, you can get aggressive with a roll crimp. If you're loading for a hard-kicking revolver like a .44 Magnum, feel free to use a good crimp! Your crimping die manufacturer will have instructions on how much adjustment you can do.

RIFLE CARTRIDGE CRIMPING

The logic of crimping, or not crimping, gets a little wonky when it comes to bottleneck rifle cartridges.

Here's why. When a bottleneck rifle cartridge is resized, the inside of the case mouth is expanded at the same time that the exterior of the case is resized. There is not a separate belling step that flares out the mouth of the case as there is with a straight

All three of these .44 Magnum cartridges use a roll crimp. The roll crimp becomes more aggressive left to right, with the lead bullet using the most crimp.

walled cartridge. The resizing opens up the entire cylindrical shaped area of the case neck evenly. Since there's not a flare at the very end, there is no need to close the flare.

So, normally, there is no need to perform a separate crimping step with a bottleneck rifle cartridge.

Normally, but not always. There are, in fact, times when you will want to use a crimp on a bottleneck rifle cartridge. Here's how to know when to apply a crimp.

If the projectile (bullet) you are using has a cannelure band, you can apply a crimp to help secure it in place, but you don't have to. You do have to crimp the mouth of the case into the cannelure groove. Since you're working with a bottleneck cartridge, you can use either a taper or roll crimp. Remember with bottleneck cartridges, the shoulder of the case is used for headspace, not the case mouth, so a roll crimp will not hurt anything.

If your bullet does not have a cannelure groove, then do not use a crimp. If you do, accuracy will suffer as you're pressing the case into the sides of the bullet and likely deforming it.

Left to right: a 5.56mm cartridge with a crimp, a .308 with a crimp and a .308 with no crimp.

You'll notice that most ammunition for military-type cartridges like 7.62x51 and 5.56mm uses aggressive crimps. That's to hold the bullets securely in place during recoil — especially when the ammo is used in automatic weapons.

The takeaway for you is fairly simple. When loading bottleneck rifle cartridges, crimp away to your hearts content if your bullets have a cannelure groove. If they don't, just adjust your seating die according to the manufacturers instructions and leave it at that.

Chapter Fifteen

INSPECTION AND PACKAGING

The very last step in the process is inspection and packaging.

After all is done, I combine the inspection and packaging steps. As I put each completed cartridge into a box, I look it over to make sure everything is in order.

Does the bullet appear to be seated at the right depth?

Are there any dents or cracks on the cartridge that I missed before?

If I'm loading lead bullets, did any lead or bullet lubricant shave off onto the outside of the cartridge case? If so, scrape it off as it will interfere with smooth chambering.

Is the bullet itself intact? Are there any dents or cuts from the seating and crimping steps?

As I put each bullet in the box, I also look at the new primer. Sometimes, a new primer won't be seated at all. Either something went wrong in the process, or perhaps that specific case had a loose primer pocket and the new primer fell out. Is the primer inserted with the proper side facing out? Once in a while, one can get turned around and seated in the primer pocket backwards.

This is your last chance before your reloads head to the range to identify any problems, so make this an important part of your routine. If you see any issues, or even have doubts about a specific cartridge, remove it. You can use a bullet puller to take it apart and start over.

I like to use plastic ammo boxes with a separate space for each completed cartridge. They look great, keep your ammo from getting knocked around and last forever. Most will come with labels so you can clearly identify the specific load you are storing. Or, you can always buy cheap stickers and put them on the outside of the container. Whatever your method, it's really important to clearly identify the exact load information of that box.

The very last step?

Go shoot it!

Chapter Sixteen

BUYING RELOADING COMPONENTS

I won't spend a lot of time talking about the details of specific components. Your reloading manual will provide plenty of detail on which specific powder, bullets and primers to buy. But there are a couple of things to understand.

BULLETS / PROJECTILES

Bullets are sold by their diameter size - not necessarily by caliber. That's because different "calibers" can share the same bullet diameter. For example, .38 Special and .357 Magnum both use bullets that are .357 inches diameter. 6.8 Remington SPC, .270 Winchester and .270 Weatherby Magnum all use bullets of .277 inches diameter. For this reason, the "standard" of labeling projectiles for reloading is generally by diameter. It's up to you to know which diameter bullet is used for a given caliber. Your reloading manual will tell you that.

You do need to follow reloading manual specifications carefully. For

Some bullets like the Hornady A-Max above, are marked with caliber and diameter. Others, like the Missouri Bullet Company semi-wadcutters below, are marked with diameter only. .452 is a common diameter lead bullet for .45 ACP cartridges.

example, identical weight lead and jacketed bullets will use different powder charges. That's because lead bullets generally take less pressure to drive through the rifling of the barrel. So don't treat different bullet materials as interchangeable.

You also might notice different load data for different shaped bullets. That's because a longer, pointier bullet and a stubbier design may weigh the same, but if you push them in from the top, the longer one will seat further into the case. So pay attention to the recipe if it specifically calls for round nose, flat points, wad cutters or whatever.

POWDER

Powder is relatively straightforward, and which one to use will be clearly specified in your reloading manual. Just be aware that some powders from different manufacturers have similar names, but they are not interchangeable. For example, you might run across Hodgdon H4895 and IMR 4895. While they are similar, load data is not interchangeable.

PRIMERS

Again, your manual will specify the exact primer type. Just be sure to read labels carefully. Significant differences might result from using large pistol magnum primers instead of regular large pistol primers. While we're on the topic, primers labeled "magnum" aren't necessarily for calibers with "magnum" in the name. They simply ignite with more fire and brimstone than regular primers. Your load recipe will tell you whether to use magnum or standard primers.

BRASS

Brass is easy if you ever need to buy empty cases for reloading. As brass cases are specific to caliber, they will be labeled clearly as such!

WHERE TO BUY YOUR COMPONENTS

You may be lucky and have a local dealer that stocks a good supply of reloading components. Or you may not. Fortunately, you can find everything you need online.

Brass and bullets generally have no shipping restrictions, but check your state and local laws. Powder and primers, however, are classified as hazardous materials, so special shipping requirements exist. You'll likely have to pay a HazMat fee in addition to standard shipping costs. Usually this is about $25. Because of the fee, it makes sense to order larger quantities of primers or powder to help amortize the cost.

Chapter Seventeen

ADVANCED EQUIPMENT

The purpose of this guide is to get you started in reloading. By understanding the basic process, equipment and principles, advanced topics will make a lot more sense when you are ready for them.

Let's take a quick look at some possible next steps in your equipment arsenal. While we won't give a comprehensive instruction set for their use, we'll give you an idea of what some of these upgrades can do to enhance your reloading experience.

RELOADING PRESSES

There are three basic types of reloading presses, each with increasing levels of automation. Of course, with more automation, your rate of production increases too. You might assume that you can create about 100 cartridges per hour with a single stage press, while a high end progressive press will let you complete up to 1,200 rounds per hour.

Since most of this book has been geared toward a single stage reloading press, let's take a look at turret and progressive presses.

Turret Reloading Presses

In the how-to chapters of this book, we addressed the most simple style of reloading press — a single stage model.

A single stage press means exactly that. It's equipped to do one single thing at a time. For that reason, single stage presses lend themselves to batch production. Rather than change dies with every cartridge you load, it's much more efficient to resize all the brass that you're going to load, then switch dies to the next operation. For example, you might do the same process, whether it be sizing, belling or seating, for 100 or more cartridges at a time. Batch production!

While production rates vary widely based on your working speed, it's safe to assume a round number of 100 cartridges per hour, give or take, with a single-stage reloading press.

A turret press is the next step up in terms of production volume because it turns batch production on its ear.

With a turret press, the top section, where you screw in the reloading die, holds multiple dies, usually four or even five. The top section, or turret, rotates and locks into each position where a die is seated, by means of

This RCBS Turret Press allows you to perform all the steps on a case by rotating the turret and dies. Image: RCBS.

handle. With a turret press, rather than do batches of one operation at a time, you can complete an entire cartridge.

The idea is to insert a cartridge case in the shell holder just as with a single stage press. After completing the sizing step, rotate the turret to the belling and/or powder drop step. Then you rotate the turret again to seat and crimp the bullet. Of course, you can still choose to do batches with a turret press, it just gives you flexibility with your workflow. A turret press might increase your rate of production to 200 cartridges per hour, give or take.

A turret press is a good way to move up the sophistication ladder. You still have to do things manually, so it's great for beginners and intermediates.

Progressive Reloading Presses

When you really get the reloading bug, and start churning out large quantities of ammunition, you'll want a progressive reloading press. Like a turret press, you mount all the dies you will use at once. Unlike a turret press, a progressive press will help fully automate the process. It will have a mechanism for seating primers and dropping powder charges in addition to the reloading die operations.

The most obvious mechanical difference between a progressive reloading press and a turret press is this: while the turret press has multiple "stations" in the turret, it only has one shell holder. A progressive reloading press has both — multiple stations for dies like a turret, but also a shell plate that holds multiple cartridge casings at once.

This is a Hornady Lock and Load Progressive Reloading press, currently set up for .308 Winchester.

Usually the shell plate and die section have the same number of positions. The idea is that the shell plate rotates and moves the cartridge case to the next station in the process. The handle on a progressive reloading press moves the entire shell plate up and down, so multiple cartridges get "worked on" with each pull of the lever. With most progressive presses, each pull of the handle results in a completed cartridge.

Some progressive reloading presses operate with manual indexing. This means that you rotate the shell plate by hand so the cartridge cases move to the next station. Others are auto-indexing, and the pull of the handle engages a ratchet which moves the shell plate to the next station automatically.

Progressive reloading presses come in various shapes, sizes and degrees of functionality. Most will have mechanisms to insert primers and drop a powder charge. Fancier ones may also have options to swage crimped primer pockets. Really fancy ones will have enough positions to mount an electric case trimmer on the press too, so all operations of cartridge reloading can be performed in one pass. Progressive presses start in the $400 range and go up to about $1,500, at which point you start to move into the realm of commercial grade reloading equipment. Take a look at offerings from RCBS, Hornady and Dillon Precision when you're ready to create your wish list!

This sounds tempting doesn't it? Why not start with a progressive reloading press from day one?

Reloading is a task of detail, where mistakes are bad. Until you really get the hang of the process, and develop an understanding of what can go wrong in the reloading process, a single stage press is the best way to start. Fortunately, you'll use your single stage press forever, no matter how sophisticated you get. They're always handy for small batches when you're testing new recipes because they are much easier to "switch over" to a different caliber than a progressive press. Start with a good single stage press and add a progressive press when you're confident and ready.

ELECTRONIC POWDER DISPENSERS

An electronic powder dispenser is an especially good tool for reloading very consistent and accurate rifle cartridges. It combines two pieces of equipment we've already discussed: a powder dispenser and an electronic scale.

They are precise and consistent because, rather than dumping a volume measure of powder that should weight a certain amount, they dispense an individually weighed powder charge each and every time.

Let's take a look at this Charge-Master Combo unit to see how an electronic powder dispenser works.

> ▷ First, fill the hopper with the powder of choice.

> ▷ Next, using the keypad on the electronic scale, enter the desired powder charge weight in grains and tenths of grains.

This RCBS ChargeMaster Combo unit dispenses and weighs each powder charge automatically.

> ▷ Hit the "Start" button and watch how the machine trickles powder into the pan on the scale until the exact weight is dispensed.

> ▷ Using a funnel, empty the pan into your cartridge case.

> ▷ Repeat!

You can even configure the RCBS ChargeMaster Combo to start dispensing the next charge when you replace the pan on the scale. While you're seating a bullet on the previous cartridge, the ChargeMaster is weighing the next charge for you.

Offerings from other manufacturers follow a similar process.

PRIMER POCKET SWAGERS

In the *Priming* chapter, we talked about the hassle of crimped primers. If you get military surplus brass, or save it from any new ammunition that had primers crimped into place, you're going to need a way to fix that before you can insert new primers. A crimp creates a rim of extra metal inside the primer pocket that has to be removed before a new one will fit in.

There are two basic ways to deal with crimped primer pockets: cutting and swaging.

As the word implies, the cutting method uses a blade from a hand-operated or electric tool to "cut" the excess metal away. This method works, but I'm not crazy about it. I find it tedious and slow.

The second method is swaging. That's a fancy word for "pushing metal back into shape." Think about it this way. If you're planting an apple seed, you could use a tiny little shovel to "cut out" a bit of dirt, thereby creating a hole for the seed. Or, you could just poke your finger into the dirt, pushing dirt out of the way, and creating a hole for the seed that way. That's the swaging method.

Here's a primer pocket swager from RCBS. Just drop a case onto the support, lower it, and press the primer pocket into shape. Image: RCBS.

High end progressive reloading presses have a swaging tool built in, so as the case advances, one step smooths out the crimped primer pocket as you go. If you don't have a high end press, you can buy a bench mounted swaging tool like the RCBS and Dillon Precision models shown here. They both work on the same basic principle. You drop a cartridge case onto a support rod, lower it into place, and using a lever, drive a swaging pin into the primer pocket. This "pushes" the crimped part of the brass primer pocket back into place.

Fortunately, primer pocket swaging is a one time thing, provided you don't get other brass mixed in to your stock, once you do it, you never have to do it again.

CASE PREP MACHINES

This primer pocket swagger from Dillion Precision makes quick work of fixing crimped primer pockets. Slip the case on the spindle (right), lower it, then pull the handle to drive a "plug" into the primer pocket and smooth out the crimp.

Earlier we talked about those nifty hand tools that help you chamfer and deburr the outside of a case after trimming.

You know there has to be an automated method of a tedious chore like that, right? And there is. A case prep machine is a lifesaver if you process a lot of bottleneck cartridges. Most, like the RCBS model shown here, have a motor that drives multiple stations. Each station will accept a variety of tools to help you chamfer, deburr, clean primer pockets, cut away the crimp from primer pockets and clean the inside of case necks.

Yes, this will spoil you rotten.

When you start processing a lot of cases, you might want to upgrade to something like this RCBS TrimMate.

POWER CASE TRIMMING

If you really, really want to be spoiled, look at power case trimmers. For small batches, the Forster Classic Case Trimmer is hard to beat. When you start cutting hundreds of rifle cartridge cases, you'll probably want to automate.

This RCBS Electric Case Trimmer is a lifesaver. It's even spring loaded so you don't have to apply hand pressure while cutting.

There are several basic styles of power case trimmers. There are bench mounted models like the RCBS case trimmer shown here. Some mount horizontally like this one, while others operate vertically. The basic operation is the same. You mount a shell in some type of shell holder, and a rotating blade guided by a collet trims the brass cartridge neck to a specified length.

Another style, like the Dillon Precision Rapid Trim Case Trimmer, actually mounts on your reloading press. After adjustment,

The RCBS cutting blade has an optional 3-way cutting head which trims the case, deburrs the outside of the cartridge mouth and chamfers the inside — all in the same operation. It's a real time saver.

you place a cartridge case in the shell holder of your press (single stage or progressive) and raise it into the trimmer. It's even got a vacuum attachment to suck away the brass shavings.

If you're going to be trimming just one or two calibers of cases, you might check out the Little Crow case trimmers. This unit fits on the end of a standard drill and is a self contained trimmer for a specific caliber. Just fasten your drill with a vise or clamp and you can push cases into the Little Crow. The adjustment is set by the case shoulder so it's not quite as precise as other methods, but it sure is simple.

The Little Crow case trimmer is an interesting solution if you only have one or two calibers to trim. It fits on the end of a standard drill. Just put your drill in a vise and insert the case mouth. Each one does one caliber and costs about $75, so if you have a lot of calibers to do, consider more general purpose options.

Each Little Crow trimmer costs about $75.

SHOOTING CHRONOGRAPH

A Shooting Chronograph is an electronic tool that measures the velocity of a bullet. Most of the current models on the market work by using two or more optical sensors to "see" the bullet passing over. The time between detection at multiple points is used to calculate velocity.

When you get serious about reloading, you really should invest in a chronograph. It's the only way to begin to know the actual performance of the loads you make. While it won't tell you pressure, it will give you hints. If velocity is higher or lower than expected, that's information you can use.

I've used a Beta Master model by Shooting Chrony for years with good success. What I like about this model is that the brains (translation: expensive part) of the unit sits safely on the shooting bench and not out there where the bullets fly. The computer circuitry, display, and controls, are connected to the sensor unit by a long cord. If you manage to hit the the expensive part of this unit, please consider some additional shooting lessons before trying again! If you chronograph ammunition long enough, you will eventually shoot the dang thing one way or another. With the Shooting Chrony Beta Master, you're only going to hit the (relatively) inexpensive parts – which are available as replacements from the manufacturer. I've managed to hit the wire sun screen supports a couple of times, but that's no big deal to replace. The Beta

Most shooting chronographs look something like this Shooting Chrony Beta Master. You shoot through the triangular areas so optical sensors can detect the bullet traveling by. Image: Shooting Chrony.

Master unit records and memorizes shot strings so you can view them at home. It also allows you to connect an optional printer for an immediate record while at the range.

New on the market is radar chronograph technology. Expected to ship very close to the time this book is scheduled for release, LabRadar offers a unit that uses radar instead of optical sensors to track velocity. It's got a couple of advantages. First, there is nothing to place down range where the bullets fly. It sits on the shooting bench and "looks" forward. Second, it can track the velocity as your bullet travels down range, out to about 100 yards or so.

Chapter Eighteen

ADVANCED TOPICS

This is an insanely practical guide, not an encyclopedia. Reloading can be an infinite topic filled with details, what-if scenarios and endless discussion and learning. That's part of the reason it's so fulfilling — there's always something new to learn. Since we can't cover everything in a starter book (and if we tried, it wouldn't be a starter book) we wanted to touch on some advanced topics.

I want you to file these away in the back of your brain, so when you encounter them on your reloading journey, you'll know to devote more research and study.

LIFE EXPECTANCY OF YOUR BRASS

Brass cartridge cases are reusable and that's what makes reloading cost effective. It's the most expensive component and you can use it anywhere from three to ten times, depending on all sorts of things.

Just be aware that you can't reload the same piece of brass indefinitely. Each time you fire and resize a piece of brass, it stretches and contracts and contains all kinds of kaboom. That gives the cartridge case a real workout over time. As a result, you need to track usage of the brass you reload, so you can dispose of it before it fails in your gun.

One thing you can do to extend the life of your brass cartridge cases is to load with moderation. As a starting reloader, I always recommend using "middle of the range" load data. Not the lowest pressure and velocity and not the highest. Your reloading manual will present a minimum starting load and a maximum, or never exceed, load. Staying in the middle zone has many benefits, especially if you're only using your reloads to poke holes in paper targets. It provides extra safety margin. It's less wear and tear on your gun. And it's less wear and tear on your brass cartridges. Using moderate power loads will allow you to use any given brass cartridge more times.

Straight wall cartridge handgun brass is pretty forgiving when it comes to reuse. It takes much less of a beating with firing and resizing than bottleneck rifle brass. As a result, it tends to last longer than rifle brass. To put that observation in perspective, a middle range .45 ACP pistol cartridge may generate 16,000 C.U.P. (Copper units of pressure) while a .308 rifle cartridge might reach 60,000 C.U.P. That's a big difference!

For standard handgun brass, I simply look for wear and tear when I inspect it in the cleaning step. If there are cracks, dents, splits, or stretch marks, it goes in the trash. If a new primer goes in too easily, then the primer pocket has been expanded and I toss those as well.

When it comes to bottleneck rifle cartridges, I perform a much more careful inspection. I'll look at the spent primer to make sure there isn't a hole all the way through it. I'll look carefully for any indications of stretching on the case, especially near the base. Any significant dent sends it to the trash. Any type of crack or split rules it out for use.

With rifle cartridges, it's also a good idea to track the number of times a case has been reloaded. You'll have to set your own limit based on how hot you load your rounds, but I never use a rifle cartridge more than ten times. If you load near the maximum load data, that number should be less. The idea is to dispose of cases before it can split or rupture.

Remember earlier in the book when I suggested you buy out the entire stock of plastic containers from your local discount store? This is a great use. For any given caliber, you might need multiple storage containers to segregate brass by the number of times it's been fired.

The important takeaway here is to understand that brass is not immortal. Track your usage accordingly and throw away brass that's served its purpose.

RELOADING FOR MILITARY SEMI-AUTOMATIC RIFLES

AR-15's are fun and just about everywhere, as are their larger cousins: M1A's, M1 Garands, M1 Carbines and other similar semi-automatic rifles. Reloading for your "battle rifle" or modern sporting rifle is fun and rewarding, and can allow you to shoot a whole lot more.

If you plan to reload for guns like this, you need to be aware of a couple of basic concepts that warrant further diligence on your part.

Guns like the M1A and AR-15 have a bolt design that allows the firing pin to "float" back and forth freely. When you fire a gun like this, a hammer smacks into the back of the firing pin, driving it forward into the primer. However, since the firing pin floats freely, it can also move forward when the semi-automatic bolt slams forward during the chambering process. On rare occasion, under the right conditions, the firing pin can move forward with enough force to ignite the primer and discharge the gun. This scenario is known as a "slam fire" as it's caused by the bolt slamming forward into battery.

Slam fires are rare, but even still, it's always a good idea to make sure your rifle is pointed down range while releasing the bolt.

I mention slam fires here as reloading techniques can increase or decrease the likelihood of a slam fire event. Some primer manufacturers, including CCI, make primers specifically designed for military style semi-automatic rifles. These primers are harder than standard and require more firing pin force to ignite. It's always a good idea to use those when reloading for semi-automatic rifles with free floating firing pins.

One other topic to quickly mention is the importance of knowing the gun for which you are reloading. A classic example is the M1 Garand chambered in .30-06. The operating system of the gun was designed for a very specific range of bullet weight, velocity and operating pressure. However, .30-06 ammunition can be bought or reloaded with a wide variety of projectile weights and velocities. Using a load that's outside of the design specification range for the M1 Garand can actually damage it by bending the operating rod.

I can't cover all such potential scenarios here. The M1 Garand just serves as a good illustration of the importance of knowing your gun and your load data. As with most all reloading topics, always check, never assume.

NECK SIZING

I didn't want to muddy up the resizing chapter with a bunny trail discussion on case neck resizing, so we'll briefly cover it here, so you know what it means and whether it applies to you.

Case neck resizing only applies to bottleneck rifle cartridges. It's a useful technique if you are reloading for a specific rifle or rifle caliber pistol like a Thompson/Center G2 Contender single shot handgun.

While the "standard" resizing operation resizes the entire case all the way down to the base, neck sizing only impacts the very end above the bottleneck area. Neck sizing will reshape the cartridge mouth area and, with an expander ball, open the case mouth neck up enough to seat a new bullet. It does not press the shoulder of the case back down like a full length resizing die.

The benefit of case neck sizing is that it's a lot easier on your brass as you're not mashing the whole case every time you resize. You're doing very little work on the brass and it will last longer.

Here's the gotcha. Part of the reason for full length resizing is to ensure that the reloaded cartridge will fit in any gun chamber for that caliber. The sides will be pressed in to proper diameter and the shoulder will be pushed back towards the base. The purpose is to create a little "play" so the cartridge will easily fit in any rifle. If you neck size only, there's a chance that your cartridge won't chamber properly in a different rifle.

But if it's for the same rifle it was fired in, the the case is already the perfect size. The pressure shapes the brass to exactly fit the chamber of your rifle — length and diameter. So if you're going to reload only for your rifle, then you don't have to worry about pushing the shoulder back into standard specs.

Make sense?

Case neck sizing works best for bolt operated rifles. Semi-automatics need a little more forgiveness with dimensions, so you're most likely better off using a standard resizing die if you're shooting a semi-automatic.

If this applies to you, experiment with case neck sizing. You might find you can improve accuracy in addition to simplifying the reloading process.

OCTAGONAL RIFLING AND LEAD BULLETS

As you dive into the reloading community, you'll almost certainly hear about loading lead bullets in Glocks or other guns that use octagonal rifling. You might also hear the more generic term polygonal rifling. Manufacturers, like Glock, will tell you not to do this. Other manufacturers who make polygonal rifled barrels don't specify the same warning.

Without going down a bunny trail on rifling technology, let's look at the basic difference. Traditional rifling looks like more of a "cut" system of grooves in the barrel. Some are in fact cut while others are pressed into shape. Whatever the manufacturing technique, the end result is similar. The grooves have abrupt sharp edges. With polygonal rifling, there are not severe cuts to form grooves. Rather, the rifling looks like gently curving hills and valleys. The theory is that the bullet makes more surface area contact with the inside of the barrel, providing for a better gas seal and improved performance.

The concern is that this type of rifling pattern can accumulate lead in the barrel more easily than traditional rifling patterns, so as you shoot lead bullets, it's possible that your barrel can start to become partially obstructed by lead deposits. It's not going to fill all the way up and close or anything, but as lead builds up, it's harder for the next bullet to get through the barrel, and pressure can increase.

All sorts of folks on the internet talk about shooting lead bullets through Glocks and other guns all the time with no claimed problems. To me, and in context of this book, it's just not worth it. You can buy plated or jacketed bullets that will avoid potential leading problems for slightly more money than lead bullets.

Since this is a beginner level book intended to introduce you to basic reloading concepts and procedures, we'll echo that recommendation. Don't use lead bullets in guns with octagonal rifling — at least until you thoroughly understand the specific gun you are reloading for and know potential issues.

Just to be clear, lead bullets are great and provide excellent results in all sorts of guns from revolvers to semi-automatic pistols to rifles. Just be aware of potential octagonal rifling issues.

Just because you can do it, doesn't mean you should. I can jump a riding lawn mower over a fire pit, but I probably shouldn't! It's hard to get into trouble obeying manufacturer recommendations.

BLACK POWDER CARTRIDGES

Black powder reloading is a completely different animal, even though many of the concepts are similar. Don't ever assume that loading data is interchangeable between black and smokeless powder recipes. Don't ever assume that you can use smokeless powder reloads in guns designed for black powder. Black powder pressures are generally far lower than those of smokeless propellant loads.

If you want to venture into the world of black powder reloading,

I recommend checking out the Lyman Products Black Powder Handbook and Reloading Manual.

STUCK CARTRIDGES: HOW TO REMOVE THEM

If you reload bottleneck cartridges that require case lubrication, you're eventually going to get one stuck in the reloading die.

As temping as it may be, don't get out the hammer and try to knock it out. There's a ridiculous amount of friction holding the brass cartridge case inside of your die, and you'll only end up bending the decapping rod in your resizing die.

Fortunately this is an easy thing to fix. You can always call your die manufacturer and tell

Yep. That's a case stuck in my resizing die. My case removal tool was broken, so I tried everything else to get it out. Hammering, sawing, flamethrower and a low-yield nuclear weapon. As you can tell, none of those approaches worked. Time to get new stuck case removal tool parts!

them your next door neighbor managed to get a cartridge case stuck in your die, and they will let you send it in for removal. This is cheap and easy, but you have to wait on the US mail until you're back in business.

Instead, you can buy a stuck case removal kit. It sounds fancy and expensive, but it's not. It's just a drill bit, thread tapping tool and a bolt with a short handle.

The idea is simple and uses that physics thing called mechanical advantage. Rather than bashing it out with brute force, you use a twisting motion to gently ease the stuck case out. The steps are simple:

  ▷ Remove the decapping / expander ball spindle from the die. With most dies, you can hold the decapping pin while twisting the top of the spindle. The decapping pin and expander ball will unscrew from the spindle and come off. When you remove the spindle, the decapping pin and ball will be knocking around inside the case, but that's OK.

This RCBS stuck case removal kit is simple and inexpensive, and will save you a lot of aggravation. Get one! Image: RCBS.

▷ Put your resizing die in a vise, or in the top of your reloading press, but upside down, so the bottom of the stuck case is facing up.

▷ Use the stuck case removal kit drill bit to drill a hole through the bottom of the stuck case, right through the primer pocket.

▷ Use the thread tap to create threads inside of the hole you just drilled. This will be easy, since brass is fairly soft.

▷ Position the spacer ring on top of your stuck case and insert the bolt into the threads you just created. Turn until the pressure pops the case out of the die. Life is good!

If you're industrious, you can buy all the parts from your local hardware store and make your own kit. But as the kit shown here is only about twenty bucks, I would order one the day you decide to reload rifle cartridges. It's a great investment in frustration prevention. And you won't have to make those embarrassing calls to your die manufacturer asking for help.

Chapter Nineteen

Parting Shots

What's Next?

As I indicated in the beginning of this book, the intent was to teach the basic steps, concepts and safety considerations of reloading your own cartridge ammunition.

If this made sense to you, and you've now got an itch to build your own ammunition, get a reloading manual that's chock full of load recipes. Most of these manuals have more technical, but incredibly informative, chapters on various aspects of reloading. If you've got the basic process down from this book, that information will make a lot more sense to you.

Here are some of the reloading manuals that I use:

Sierra Rifle and Handgun Loading Data
Lyman Reloading Handbook
Hornady Handbook of Cartridge Reloading
Barnes Bullets Reloading Manual

Keep In Touch!

We hope you enjoyed reading this book. Our goal is to get you started in reloading while avoiding some of the complexity and intimidation.

Be sure to pay attention to the safety tips. Reloading is a safe and enjoyable hobby provided you exercise caution and faithfully stick to published reloading data and procedures.

Now go have fun!

If you liked the book, please leave a review at the book seller where you purchased it. I make my living writing books and every review really makes a difference. If you didn't find the book useful, I would also like to hear from you. Just drop me an email at tom@insanelypracticalguides.com.

One more thing. Stay in touch by subscribing to our email list. We send updates on books, shooting tips and other fun news once a week, with no spam ever!

Sign up here: mygunculture.com/email

About the Author

Tom is the primary author of the Insanely Practical Guides series of how-to books. He believes that shooting can be safe and fun, and works hard to make the shooting world easy to under-stand. If you want to learn about the world of guns, shooting and the American way, check out some of his books. Have a laugh or two. Life is too short for boring "how to" books.

You can find print and ebook versions at Amazon. For more information, check out InsanelyPracticalGuides.com

Feel free to visit Tom at his website, MyGunCulture.com. It's a half-cocked but right on target look at the world of shooting and all things related. If you want to learn with a laugh about guns, shooting products, personal defense, competition, industry news and the occasional Second Amendment issue, visit him there.

Drop me an email at: tom@insanelypracticalguides.com

Or stay in touch with our social media sites:
www.facebook.com/mygunculture
www.twitter.com/mygunculture
www.pinterest.com/mygunculture
https://plus.google.com/+TomMcHale

ALSO FROM INSANELY PRACTICAL GUIDES

If you own a Springfield Armory XD-S, or are thinking about buying one, then this book is for you! In insanely practical fashion, we cover everything you need to know about the Springfield Armory XD-S pocket pistol family. Whether 9mm, .45 ACP or the new 4.0 model — we show you how to safely use, maintain and accessorize your Springfield Armory XD-S. Using light-hearted and plain English style, we provide easy to understand tips and advice.

If you're thinking about buying a gun, are new to shooting, or just haven't immersed yourself in the gun culture, guns and shooting can be intimidating! Loud noises, armed people and gun stores can be scary. Never fear! This book will make you comfortable, and knowledgeable, in no time. And you'll have a few laughs in the process.

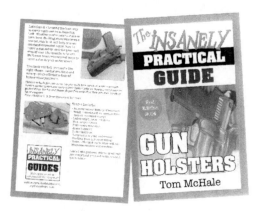

Choosing the best way to carry a gun can be a daunting task. Whether you're new to guns or have been shooting since you were a wee tot, this book can help you understand concealed carry methods, how to carry a gun safely, and the relative pros and cons of over 150 specific holster models. We'll even teach you several ways to carry a gun in your underwear. This book will help you make the right choice — saving you time and money — while offering a dose of humor while you learn.

Find information on our books at InsanelyPracticalGuides.com

CPSIA information can be obtained at www.ICGtesting.com
Printed in the USA
LVOW08s2134081014

407963LV00011B/253/P